Search and Rescue

Patrick Madrid

Search and Rescue

How to Bring Your Family and Friends
into — or Back into —
the Catholic Church

Foreword by Scott Hahn

SOPHIA INSTITUTE PRESS®
Manchester, New Hampshire

Sophia Institute Press®
Box 5284, Manchester, NH 03108
1-800-888-9344
www.sophiainstitute.com

Library of Congress Cataloging-in-Publication Data
Madrid, Patrick, 1960-
    Search and rescue : how to bring your family and friends into, or
back into, the Catholic Church / Patrick Madrid.
        p.   cm.
    ISBN 1-928832-27-X (pbk. : alk. paper)
    1. Evangelistic work. 2. Catholic Church — Membership. I. Title.

BX2347.4.M33 2001
248'.5'08822 — dc21   2001020743

06 07 10 9 8

To my friend David Hess.

We once were blind, but now we see.

"Evangelize always.
When necessary, use words."

St. Francis of Assisi

Contents

Foreword

Ever since I left the Protestant ministry to come home to the Catholic Church, I've marveled at how effectively secularism and materialism — not to mention tireless missionaries from non-Catholic and non-Christian groups — have steadily drawn people out of the Church Jesus founded. I've also met Catholics who think that evangelization is not really for Catholics; it's just a weird custom practiced by Fundamentalists, Mormons, Jehovah's Witnesses, and other enthusiasts.

Yet Jesus didn't only call others to "make disciples of all nations";[1] He called Catholics. Indeed, He called you and me. That means that it's time for us to learn how to search for and rescue our family and friends who are outside the Church and free them from the grip of error.

You know, the loss when a soul leaves the Church is incalculable; but great is the rejoicing in Heaven when a

[1] Matt. 28:19.

Search and Rescue

sinner repents.[2] You and I need to bring back fallen-away Catholics and to help our Father bring new sheep into His fold. When we do so, we obey His command to make disciples and we show our gratitude to Him for the immeasurable gift of His Church.

In *Search and Rescue*, Patrick Madrid teaches you the best methods for bringing people into the Catholic Church — methods drawn from Scripture, the wisdom of the saints, and plain old common sense.

What I like most about *Search and Rescue* is that it's not merely another arsenal of answers to questions that non-Catholics raise. There are plenty of answer books out there already, and I'm grateful for them: they provide a service for Catholics that can't be underestimated.

But they're not enough!

In *Search and Rescue*, Patrick provides what many of those books lack: the spiritual elements that must be there if you're ever to win converts to the Faith.

That's because people can't be won over by intellectual arguments alone. God created us in His image as a marvelous unity of spirit, soul, and body. Our intellect is only one component in our decision-making process.

[2] Cf. Luke 15:7.

Apostles who have all the answers but do not love often just drive their hearers away from the Church.

When I was a Protestant minister I valued words and the realities they signified, and as a professor of Catholic theology, I still do. But as a husband, a father, and a child of God, I know from long experience that my best sermons are preached, my best lessons are taught, and my best messages are sent with no words at all. That's why St. Francis of Assisi admonished us to "evangelize always. When necessary, use words."

St. Francis's advice may seem paradoxical to you, but it distills the wisdom that the Church and her saints have learned from two thousand years of successful evangelizing. Relying on this principle, the Church swelled from twelve Apostles in Palestine to hundreds of millions of Catholics around the world today.

In *Search and Rescue*, Patrick Madrid explains for you this basic principle of evangelization and shows you how to make it a part of your daily life. Soon you, too, will be evangelizing — effectively — your family and friends; when necessary, you'll even be using words.

Scott Hahn
Spring 2001

Introduction

"God has created me to do Him
some definite service;
He has committed some work to me
which He has not committed to another.
I have my mission."

John Henry Cardinal Newman

For nearly fifteen years now, as a Catholic apologist, I've traveled the globe preaching the Catholic Faith, in person, on the radio, and on television; I've engaged in formal debates on the Catholic Church with Protestant ministers in Protestant churches; I've written many articles and books defending the Faith and explaining why all men and women should be Catholic. I've been in countless small-group and one-on-one discussions with non-Catholics and former Catholics, trying to convince them to come home to the Catholic Church.

Given that experience, you'd think that by now I would have managed to bring all my friends and family members into — or back into — the Catholic Church.

Not so!

And that's one of my greatest sorrows: although I can draw to Christ the souls of strangers, I sometimes find myself unable even to get a hearing from some of those I love the most.

I'm not alone.

Search and Rescue

In my travels, I've met thousands of other Catholics
in my situation; and it's likely that you, too, are numbered
among us: heartbroken because someone near and dear to
you has left the Church or refuses to consider entering it; a
son, a daughter, a coworker, or a close friend.

This book is for you . . . and for those you love who are
outside the Church.

In it, I'm going to share with you what I've learned from
my own mistakes and successes, and from those with whom
I've spent long hours discussing this difficult problem: how
can those of us who dearly love Christ and His Church bring
into the Church those we love most of all?

Regardless of how successful we may be in other areas, I
don't think that you and I can turn away from this personal
evangelizing task, or leave it to be done by others.

Probably these first paragraphs have brought to your own
mind a number of people: perhaps your sister-in-law Jennifer
who left the Church last year in anger over a sermon that
she thought was too harsh; maybe Bob from the front office
who brings up religion in the lunchroom but whom you
seem only to drive more deeply into Protestant Fundamentalism; maybe even your husband or wife, to whom
you can't be as close as you want because of a difference
of religion.

Introduction

There's a reason these particular people came to mind: they've been put into your life by God's mysterious Providence. From all eternity, He has marked out for you a role to play in His plan of salvation. Regardless of your circumstances — in your office, your home, your social circles, or your parish — God wants to work through you; He wants you to search out these friends and family members whose souls are in danger because they have drifted or are drifting away from the Catholic Faith; He wants you to be His instrument to rescue them.

Although your temperament, abilities, and circumstances are unique, God wants to make *you* His coworker in the vast drama of salvation. He's calling on you to play a vital role — to undertake a spiritual search-and-rescue mission — and I'm writing this book to show you how to do it.

In these pages I'll acquaint you with proven techniques from the Church's two thousand years of wisdom and experience that will help you do three things better:

• Explain your Catholic Faith more intelligently;
• Defend it more charitably; and
• Share it more effectively

so that through your prayers, your words, and your example, you'll draw your family and friends closer to Jesus in His Catholic Church.

Search and Rescue

I know that whether you're a housewife, a dentist, a student, a retired person, a factory worker, a butcher, a baker, or a candlestick maker, you can effectively bring your loved ones into — or back into — a close relationship with Christ and His Church.

Right here, right now, you already have all the tools you need for your search-and-rescue mission. All you have to do is use them.

In this book, I'll show you how.

Patrick Madrid
Spring 2001

Search and Rescue

Chapter 1

Let love fill your heart

"First let a little love find entrance
into their hearts,
and the rest will follow."

St. Philip Neri

The key to success in your own search-and-rescue mission lies in the quiet recesses of your own heart: love. To win your family and friends to the Faith, you must develop the heart of an apostle (one who is sent) — a heart full of love for Christ and for souls.

St. Francis de Sales[3] had such a heart, and the love burning in it enabled him to win many converts, drawing back into the Church of their fathers over sixty thousand anti-Catholic souls who had earlier rejected the Church for Calvinism.

St. Francis had volunteered for an arduous pastoral assignment in the Chablais region of southeastern France, which was close to Geneva and sixty years earlier had been largely converted to Protestantism by John Calvin. The Catholic Church had recently been allowed to re-establish herself, but uprooting the entrenched hatred of Catholicism

[3] 1567-1622.

was extraordinarily difficult. Yet that's exactly what young
Francis de Sales volunteered to do.

To avoid the hostility of the local people, St. Francis
often traveled by night, even in harsh weather. Getting
soaked, chilled, and even chased away became a way of life
for him. He actually spent one night secured by his belt to
a tree branch, safely out of reach of a pack of dogs that had
been set on him by an anti-Catholic farmer. That's just one
of many such "adventures" he endured cheerfully and out
of love for Christ as he carried out his search-and-rescue
mission.

In his 1923 encyclical *Rerum omnium perturbationem*,
Pope Pius XI wrote with admiration about St. Francis de
Sales:

> He was accustomed to repeat to himself, as a source
> of inspiration, that well-known phrase "Apostles bat-
> tle by their sufferings and triumph only in death." It
> is almost unbelievable with what vigor and constancy
> he defended the cause of Jesus Christ among the peo-
> ple of La Chablais. In order to bring them the light
> of faith and the comforts of the Christian religion, he
> was known to have traveled through deep valleys and
> to have climbed steep mountains. If they fled him, he

pursued, calling after them loudly. Repulsed brutally, he never gave up the struggle; when threatened he only renewed his efforts. He was often put out of lodgings, at which times he passed the night asleep on the snow under the canopy of heaven. He would celebrate Mass though no one would attend. When, during a sermon, almost the entire audience one after another left the Church, he would continue preaching. At no time did he ever lose his mental poise or his spirit of kindness toward these ungrateful hearers. It was by such means as these that he finally overcame the resistance of his most formidable adversaries.[4]

St. Francis de Sales could do these things with joy and perseverance because he trusted God to guide and support him. He once wrote: "In all your affairs, rely entirely on the Providence of God through which alone all your plans succeed. . . . Strive very gently to cooperate with it. Then, believe that if you trust well in God success will come to you."[5]

You need to develop this same attitude of trust in your own efforts to help others come home to the Church.

---

[4] Pius XI, *Rerum omnium perturbationem*, sect. 8.

[5] St. Francis de Sales, *Introduction to the Devout Life*, Pt. 3, ch. 10.

Search and Rescue

St. Francis's ministry in the towns and hamlets near Geneva was especially challenging. The area had become so entrenched in Calvinist anti-Catholicism that few people would gather for the sermons he preached in the town square; his Masses were poorly attended. Aside from a few recent converts and those hardy Catholics who had managed to weather the decades-long Calvinist winter and remain true to the Church, no one was willing to listen to his arguments in favor of Catholicism. And it wasn't that St. Francis was particularly inept: other priests had come before him and tried to gain a foothold for the Church there, but most had left soon afterward, defeated by their inability to get through to the people.

If these facts sound like the discouraging results you've achieved in trying to evangelize your family and friends, then read on.

⌒

You must develop the virtues of an apostle

St. Francis knew that his mission of evangelization could be accomplished. He knew that, if he remained faithful to his apostolate, God would provide the graces necessary for the true Faith to flourish once again within the hearts of these good people.

What was it that sustained St. Francis in his difficult search-and-rescue mission, when others had given up?

He had developed the virtues that flow from an apostle's heart — a heart full of love for Christ. It is these virtues that you and I must also develop if we are to bring our family and friends into the Church:

- *Prayer:* St. Francis knew that he could win no souls without prayerful reliance on God. Being faithful in prayer allowed God's grace to well up within him and flow forth, reaching untold numbers of people.

  To win souls to Christ, you must grow faithful in prayer. Remember the example of St. Monica, the mother of St. Augustine: when she complained to a bishop that Augustine would not listen to her admonitions that he become a Catholic, the bishop urged her, "Speak less to Augustine about God and more to God about Augustine." When you're working to convert someone, do the same. It works!

- *Absolute trust in God:* Measured by human standards, the task of winning sixty thousand Calvinists back to the Faith seemed to be impossible. But St. Francis trusted in Christ's words: "What is impossible with men is possible with God."[6] He knew that God's

---

[6] Luke 18:27.

grace could melt even the hardest hearts. He wasn't daunted, therefore, by the seemingly impregnable resistance to the Church he saw in the people he had come to evangelize.

The greater your trust in God, the better you'll be able to carry out your own work of evangelization.

• *Humility:* In his search-and-rescue mission, St. Francis saw countless conversions, not as a result of his own clever preaching, but because of the power and mercy of God. What God needed was someone to take His message to the people,[7] and St. Francis recognized that he was merely the messenger.

Remember that the messenger is subordinate to the message: this will help keep you humble. The task and the success, if any, will never be yours alone. On the contrary, God is merely using you as His instrument to do His will in the world.

• *Perseverance:* As St. Francis would relate in later years, it was his reliance on God and his commitment to daily prayer and the sacraments that enabled him to carry out his difficult apostolic work. His fidelity to

[7] Cf. Rom. 10:14-18.

the little things in his daily life, especially fidelity to prayer (even when he didn't feel like praying), was his loving response to Christ's words: "He who is faithful in a very little is faithful also in much; and he who is dishonest in a very little is dishonest also in much."[8]

Resolve to be faithful and persevere in small matters, even when you're discouraged. Be kind, be polite, and say your prayers. God will make up for what you lack.

• *Love:* Above all, St. Francis was a model of charity, kind and helpful to all he encountered, in spite of the indifference, the anti-Catholic scorn, and the physical threats he faced, even when he felt exasperated or angry. He didn't set out on his search-and-rescue mission to win arguments or to accumulate converts as if they were trophies; on the contrary, he had a deep love for those he was sent to evangelize. He recognized them for what they were: his brothers and sisters; men and women who were loved by Christ, but who had drifted away from the fullness of the true Faith. He loved them with the love of Christ — not in a superior or haughty way, but with the humble love of a man who goes in

---

[8] Luke 16:10.

search of a lost brother. By the grace of God, his self-less love for others eventually yielded a vast crop of good fruit.

You, too, must never look upon those you evangelize as trophies, as yet more converts to be won; look upon each of them tenderly, as your brothers and sisters, and they soon will sense your tenderness and their hard hearts will melt.

⸎

The heart of an apostle wins souls

Francis realized that his preaching and good example weren't sufficient to persuade the intransigent non-Catholics he had worked so hard to win to the Church. His circumstances required ingenuity, so Francis, through prayer, developed a method for sharing the Faith in a way that proved to be extremely effective. He knew that the good Protestant folks of the Chablais region had for decades been taught by government and religious authorities to reject and even fear the Catholic religion. Negative "peer pressure" was regularly exerted on those who were curious enough about the message of this new Catholic priest to make them want to attend his conferences. Many stayed away simply because they didn't want to be reproached by neighbors. Recognizing this problem, Francis changed his methods.

Each week, he composed and printed a brief apologetics essay on an issue that separated Catholics and Protestants, topics such as the Eucharist, the authority of the Church, the infallibility of the Pope, Mary, and the sacraments. In these essays, he offered simple but convincing biblical explanations for these Catholic teachings, and he took great care to respond charitably to the standard objections to them raised by the Protestant ministers who opposed him. Early in the morning, before the townspeople got up, Francis slipped his tracts under the door of each home, Catholic and Protestant. He knew that if, free from peer pressure, the people could just read for themselves the biblical and historical case for the Catholic Church, they would be more likely to consider the Catholic message. And that's precisely what happened.

After just four years, through Francis de Sales's personal sanctity, preaching, writing, and reaching out to those around him with unselfish charity and genuine Christ-like love, God began to work a miracle of grace.

Conversions began.

At first they were scattered and intermittent, but within months the trickle turned into a steady stream. Within a few years, it was a flood. By the time St. Francis died in 1622, more than sixty thousand former Protestants had converted to the Catholic Church through the efforts of St. Francis.

Search and Rescue

Many prominent Calvinist theologians and ministers were among those brought to the Catholic Faith by the gentle apostolic zeal of this holy priest.

$\Longrightarrow$

Even if you have few talents, you can rely on love

You may be thinking to yourself, "Yes, Francis de Sales was impressive, but I'm not like him. He had a gift for explaining the Faith and bringing people into the Church. I don't. He was a priest, he was trained for that sort of thing, and he lived hundreds of years ago when things weren't nearly so complicated as they are now. And besides, he was a *saint* — I'm definitely not."

Your reaction is understandable, but the fact that you picked up this book in the first place and have read this far shows that on some level, you feel the need to speak of the faith to someone close to you. Say with confidence and joyful humility, "I can do all things in Him who strengthens me."[9] That was precisely the attitude of St. Francis de Sales, and you must make it your own. St. Francis knew he could never make headway among the Calvinists unless he relied on Christ for his strength and guidance. In spite of his intellect, his gift for writing, and his many other talents, St.

[9] Phil. 4:13.

Francis de Sales's success as a search-and-rescue evangelist was, ultimately, not a result of his own talents.

Let me repeat that point for maximum impact: his being clever, well-spoken, and a master theologian was not responsible for his success in making converts. Someone with few intellectual gifts and minimal social grace could also have accomplished such a mission of converting souls to Christ, and in the history of the Church, many such people have done so.[10]

Blessed Josemaría Escrivá, founder of Opus Dei, knew the key to converting souls to Christ: "Treat those who are in error with loving kindness, with Christian charity."[11] St. Francis de Sales knew this, too. He was able to win souls to the Church because he had the heart of an apostle. None of his advantages would have amounted to anything substantial in his mission had he not possessed a burning love for Christ

---

[10] A perfect example is St. John Vianney (1786-1859), the simple country priest known as the *Curé d'Ars*. Intellectually and socially, he was considered a dunce. He flunked out of the seminary and was ordained to the priesthood only because of the pity of a kindly bishop. Yet he burned with love for Christ and for others. In spite of his meager intellect, his charity gave him an amazing ability to reach even hardened sinners with the love of Christ. He was able to draw thousands into or back into the Church.

[11] Blessed Josemaría Escrivá, *The Forge* (London: Scepter Press, 1988), no. 863.

and for his neighbor, a love that radiated and warmed those around him. This wellspring of charity (purely a gift of God's grace) animated all his actions and made effective his efforts to spread the kingdom of Christ.

This key that gave him success lies within your own reach. It's the grace and virtue of supernatural charity — love. That's what dwells within the heart of an apostle; with prayer, it can dwell within your heart, too.

All the tools and techniques that I discuss in later chapters, all the principles and maxims I mention, will be useful to you (and to God) — and your own search-and-rescue mission will be successful — only if you make a conscious, daily effort to love others with the heart of an apostle. St. Thérèse of Lisieux knew this: ". . . Love was the true motive force that enabled the other members of the Church to act; if it ceased to function, the Apostles would forget to preach the gospel, the Martyrs would refuse to shed their blood."[12]

St. Paul, the greatest evangelist of all, identified love as the virtue above all that an effective evangelist must have:

> If I speak in the tongues of men and of angels, but
> have not love, I am a noisy gong or a clanging cymbal.

[12] Paul Thigpen, A *Dictionary of Quotes from the Saints* (Ann Arbor: Servant Publications, 2001), 136.

And if I have prophetic powers, and understand all mysteries and all knowledge, and if I have all faith, so as to move mountains, but have not love, I am nothing. If I give away all I have, and if I deliver my body to be burned [i.e., for martyrdom], but have not love, I gain nothing.[13]

Never forget this admonition from St. Paul; without love, your search-and-rescue mission cannot succeed.

Ask yourself now

• Do I pray daily?

• Do I recognize that God is the only One who can convert souls, and that I'm only His instrument, to be used as He chooses?

• Am I prepared to persist in my efforts to win my loved one to Christ, even if it takes years?

Search-and-rescue action agenda

• Devote as much time to praying for those you hope to bring into the Church as you do to speaking to them.

[13] 1 Cor. 13:1-3.

Search and Rescue

• Meditate on St. Paul's words on love in 1 Corinthians 13.

• Resolve to try to love others as fervently as you try to convert them.

• End your meditations and resolutions with the following prayer:

O my God,
I love Thee above all things,
with my whole heart and soul,
because Thou art all good
and worthy of all love.
I love my neighbor as myself
for the love of Thee.
I forgive all who have injured me
and ask pardon of all whom I have injured.

Chapter 2

☞

Do it for God, not for victory

"Let each one remember that he will
make progress in all spiritual things
only insofar as he rids himself of
self-love, self-will, and self-interest."

St. Ignatius of Loyola

Your ego is a dangerous thing, and egoism is a trap that's easy for you to fall into once you launch your search-and-rescue mission for souls. Not having a tight grip on your ego can be far worse than being scripturally unprepared. Your ego, if uncontrolled, will quickly distort your search-and-rescue mission into a search-and-destroy mission. I've seen it happen many times.

In this chapter, I'll give you tips for curbing your ego when you share the Faith with your friends and family. I'll also show you how to deal with another's ego when it gets in the way of his ability or willingness to understand and embrace the truth.

Your ego makes you put yourself first

The ego is that part of each of us that says, "I! Me! My!" in relation and in reaction to the world around us. Since you and I can perceive the world only from our own, unique vantage point, the ego is a natural part of who we are as human beings. We see everything and everyone in relation to that single fixed point of reference: ourselves.

Now, even though it's in our nature as individuals to see things this way, we still have to guard against the egocentric tendencies we all have. In this respect, the ego is no different from other natural elements in our soul, such as eating and drinking (which we have to govern, or we'll quickly fall into the sins of gluttony and drunkenness[14]).

The ego can fall into the bad habit of seeing everything outside us as revolving around us. This tendency to want others to revolve around us can be dangerous, especially when it gets tangled up with our desire to bring Christ to those around us.

An unchecked ego is like a weed that grows up around the heart and chokes off its ability to be selfless and seek the good of others. In the heart of an "I! Me! My!" person, other people and their needs are secondary at best. This is deadly for you as a Christian, because it prevents you from fulfilling Christ's command that you restrain your ego and seek the good of those around you. "A new commandment I give to you, that you love one another; even as I have loved you, that you also love one another. By this all men will know

[14] Cf. Prov. 20:1, 23:21; Isa. 5:11; Eph. 5:18.

22

that you are my disciples, if you have love for one another."[15]
To obey this commandment, especially as it pertains to your
search-and-rescue efforts, you have to let go of your ego.

An unchecked ego will also cause pain and privation for
your family, friends, and coworkers. It will blind you to their
needs: you'll be concerned only about the things you want.
St. Paul warned against this: "Do nothing from selfishness or
conceit, but in humility count others better than yourselves.
Let each of you look not only to his own interests, but also
to the interests of others."[16]

Examine your motive

Vainglory — that self-serving, self-admiring attitude that
your ego wants so strongly to foster in you — is a self-imposed
straitjacket for the search-and-rescue apostle. If you want to
be free to reach out to your non-Catholic friends and relatives
with the truth about Christ, you mustn't give in to vainglory.
Here's what a wise priest once wrote about it:

> Vainglory is an expression of envy and jealousy and,
> therefore, an obstacle to brotherly love. Vainglory is
> an inordinate regard of self. It is self-conceit, the

[15] John 13:34-35.
[16] Phil. 2:3-4.

overestimation of one's powers — social position, learning or talent, or skill or ability. . . .

St. Paul considers vainglory an obstacle to brotherly love. "Love is not arrogant, or rude. Love does not insist on its own way." Anyone who permits himself to be governed by vainglory easily arouses resentment in others. . . .

Try to see how vainglory tends to belittle the good you do possess; how it tends to make you untrue, unhappy, and ridiculous in the eyes of others; how it spoils your character. You have received great favors and unmerited blessings from God. Of yourself, you are and have nothing, except sin. Left to yourself, you would be a slave to passion. Whatever is good in you is really due to the working of grace in your soul. Therefore, humility and gratitude should be natural to you.[17]

Pause and let those words of wisdom sink into your soul. Now think for a moment about the non-Catholics in your life with whom you'd really like to be able to share the Faith, but who seem resistant to you, closed off, unwilling to listen.

[17] Lawrence G. Lovasik, *The Hidden Power of Kindness* (Manchester, New Hampshire: Sophia Institute Press, 1999), 65-66.

Do it for God, not for victory

Ask yourself these questions:

• Am I a victim of my own ego and vainglory? Do I honestly seek the good of the other person, or do I want to convert him because it will make me feel better about myself?

• Do I approach my non-Catholic friends and family with a contentious spirit? Am I defensive or argumentative when the subject of religion comes up?

• Am I courteous? Am I considerate? Do I realize that those around me are not necessarily able to see the Catholic Church objectively, and that their lack of objectivity may not be their own fault? Does their inability to accept the Church irritate me, or does it cause me to be more patient and considerate with them?

• What are my real motives for wanting to bring my non-Catholic friends into the Catholic Church? Deep down, do I want to win arguments or to win souls?

• Do I have (or am I striving to cultivate) a sincere spirit of detachment? Do I think I'm a failure in God's eyes because I haven't been successful in bringing someone home to the Catholic Church? Have I lost my interior peace and serenity and become agitated or irritable over these situations?

These are just some of the questions you should ask yourself and God in prayer. It's crucial that you examine your motives, check your ego, and make a strong, consistent effort to seek the good of those around you, even if that means you may need to be silent in the face of ridicule or obstinacy toward the Catholic Church or yourself.

Think often of the words of Blessed Josemaría Escrivá: "For all your learning, all your fame, all your eloquence and power, if you're not humble, you're worth nothing. Cut out that ego that dominates you so completely — root it out. God will help you. And then you'll be able to begin to work for Christ in the lowest place in His army of apostles."[18]

~

Don't let your ego drive people away from the Church

Let me tell you about three men I know and how each of them dealt with their egos in trying to convert others. Two of these men are Catholic; one is Protestant.

"Skip" is a lifelong Catholic who became interested in apologetics several years ago. At first, explaining and

---

[18] Blessed Josemaría Escrivá, *The Way* (New Rochelle, New York: Scepter Press, 1985), no. 602.

defending the Faith was a pastime, but eventually he became engrossed in it and devoted all his spare time to "converting" Protestants. He became a victim of his own vainglory. He came to see non-Catholics as potential trophies. For Skip, getting non-Catholics to say yes to the Catholic Church became an obsession. He took advantage of every chance he got to buttonhole Protestants and batter them with Bible verses and historical arguments in support of the Catholic Church.

Skip became reasonably skilled at arguing on behalf of the Church, and soon his appetite for winning arguments became insatiable. He classified all non-Catholics in the world into two categories: the ones he had converted, and the ones he hadn't converted yet.

Most non-Catholics found Skip's "clutch and grab" style of apologetics to be obnoxious, and his potential converts realized quickly that his goal was merely to win arguments. He'd drop anything at any time to ply a potential convert with books or tapes or to hold long phone conversations aimed at convincing them of the error of their non-Catholic religion. But he seemed to go to these lengths solely to stoke the fires of his own ego. Every person he won to the Catholic Church was a "win" for him.

Skip's problem was that he wasn't a search-and-rescue apostle; he was a search-and-destroy big-game trophy hunter.

Search and Rescue

He won arguments, but in the process, because he lost sight of why he was doing this in the first place, he drove many people farther from the Church by his ego-ridden quest to rack up more "points."

The second man I'll call William. He's an Evangelical Protestant who works hard to convince Catholics that they're in a heretical, counterfeit Christian system. Unlike Skip, William doesn't chase after opportunities to get into religious arguments with others. He's more discriminating and follows through only in situations in which he's likely to receive public praise and admiration for his efforts to convert Catholics. William's cleverness and his gift for rhetoric and quick thinking have helped him rise to a level of public visibility, where he's lauded by his followers and vilified by many of his opponents.

His problem, like Skip's, is ego — he has a self-conceit that blinds him to the way he comes across to those he so badly wants to convert. If charity and a sincere love for others were at the core of his efforts to convert Catholics, he would make more headway. Fortunately, though, his efforts to draw Catholics out of the Church are blunted, almost entirely, simply because his ego turns people off.

Finally, there's "Michael." A former Evangelical Protestant minister who's now Catholic, he isn't like William or Skip in the area of the ego. Michael radiates a genuine, sincere, Christ-like love for those around him. He has a deep spirit of detachment in his efforts to explain and share the Catholic Faith. He strives to help others come closer to Christ and the Church, not for selfish or vainglorious reasons, not to win arguments (although he's a formidable apologist), but because he knows that he's called by Christ to sow the seed and then move forward. He knows that the reason for the conversion of anyone he helps bring to the Faith is God's grace, not his own powers of persuasion or argumentation.

True, Michael sometimes feels anxiety and concern for others, especially when he has worked hard to provide them with biblical and historical evidence for Catholicism and they don't accept it. But he knows better than to imagine that the whole process of conversion is riding on his shoulders alone. He knows that God is working on these other people through unseen, mysterious channels of grace. He's detached because his motives are genuine: he isn't doing this to build up his ego; he's seeking the greater good of others.

These three men show why it's so important for you to guard against your ego when you engage in search-and-rescue missions to your non-Catholic family and friends.

Search and Rescue

Skip is a wannabe apostle who has the zeal but lacks the charity that would transform his efforts from a head-hunting expedition into a search-and-rescue mission. He talks to others about the Faith because doing so satisfies his deep-seated appetite for winning arguments.

William has skill and dedication, but he's at the mercy of his pride. He's like some of the non-Catholics you'll sometimes encounter in your search-and-rescue mission. Keep in mind two things here. First, William's smug conceit makes it very hard, if not impossible, for him to lure Catholics out of the Church (for them, this is a good thing), because they're repelled by his inflated ego. Don't be like him as you reach out to your non-Catholic family and friends. He's the opposite of the kind of apostle you must be. He's proud of himself; you must be humble. He's haughty and condescending; you must be genuine and personable. He's ineffective because his ego has wrapped its tentacles around him, constricting his efforts. By avoiding those pitfalls, you'll be effective at winning people over to the truth.

The second thing to remember about William is that Christ loves him and wants to rescue him as much as He does anyone else. William himself is a wandering sheep (although he doesn't realize it and would never admit it if he did). So you must learn from him how to approach those in your own life who are like him. No doubt you can think of a family member or a friend — whether he's a former Catholic, a Protestant, or even a non-Christian — whose attitude toward the Catholic Church resembles William's. You want to draw that person closer to the truth, but he won't come; he has become so inflated with his own sense of brilliance and self-importance that he can't allow anyone, least of all you, to show him he's wrong about anything. My advice is that in cases like this, you must approach the person primarily through prayer. Definitely look for opportunities to explain the Faith to him, but be much more reliant on your hidden "secret weapons" of prayer and fasting on his behalf.[19]

Now let's look at Michael again. He isn't out to win arguments. He's looking for the greater good of those around him. That's why he's an effective search-and-rescue apostle.

Imitate Michael. Examine your own motives often, and work for the good of souls, not for your own good. By controlling your ego and developing a spirit of humility, you'll

---

[19] When faced with an obstinate evil spirit who plagued a boy, the Apostles asked Jesus, "Why could we not cast it out?" Jesus answered, "This kind cannot be driven out by anything but prayer and fasting" (Mark 9:28-29: some translations omit "and fasting"; cf. Tobit 5:8; Jon. 3:5-10; Matt. 6:16-18).

not only avoid obstacles in your search-and-rescue mission, but you'll also draw others to the Faith by your genuine concern for them. Concentrate on being a sower of the seed of truth, leaving in God's hands whether your next-door neighbor will accept or reject that truth. Always be ready, willing, and able to "make a defense to anyone who calls you to account for the hope that is in you, yet do it with gentleness and reverence."[20]

Ask yourself now

• What are my motives for wanting to draw others to the Faith? Do I want to win souls or to win arguments?

• Am I kind and courteous in approaching others about the Faith?

• Have I commended to God my search-and-rescue mission — and its apparent successes or failures?

---

[20] 1 Pet. 3:15. An excellent tool to help you cultivate that attitude of gentleness and reverence is *The Hidden Power of Kindness*, by Lawrence G. Lovasik. Read it once a year to help you keep your ego in check and deepen your humility. (For more information on this book and others recommended in these pages, see the reading plan at the end of this book.)

Do it for God, not for victory

Search-and-rescue action agenda

• Examine your motives frequently, asking God to help you find and root out any vainglory, selfishness, or anger in you.

• Go to Confession regularly, and particularly keep in mind sins of vainglory and pride.

• Receive Communion weekly, or even daily; ask Christ in the Eucharist to help you keep your ego in check.

• Forget about slights and insults immediately. (I know this is easy to say and hard to do, but God will grant you this grace if you ask Him to.)

• Meditate often on these words of St. Paul: "Put on then, as God's chosen ones, holy and beloved, compassion, kindness, lowliness, meekness, and patience, forbearing one another and, if one has a complaint against another, forgiving each other; as the Lord has forgiven you, so you also must forgive. And above all these put on love, which binds everything together in perfect harmony. And let the peace of Christ rule in your hearts."[21]

[21] Col. 3:12-15.

Search and Rescue

• Remind yourself often that you're God's messenger.
Commend your search-and-rescue mission to Him.
Read Thomas à Kempis, *Imitation of Christ*, Book 3,
Chapters 8-9.

• End your meditations and resolutions with the
following prayer:

> Who can discern his errors?
> Clear Thou me from hidden faults.
> Keep back Thy servant also
> from presumptuous sins;
> let them not have dominion over me!
> Then I shall be blameless,
> and innocent of great transgression.
> Let the words of my mouth and
> the meditation of my heart
> be acceptable in Thy sight, O Lord,
> my Rock and my Redeemer.[22]

---

[22] Ps. 19:12-14.

Chapter 3

∼

Use prayer and example to draw
friends and family to Christ

"May your behavior and your conversation be such
that everyone who sees or hears you can say:
This man reads the life of Jesus Christ."

Blessed Josemaría Escrivá

⌒

God's grace and your authentic Christian example can do more to win souls for Christ than all the biblical or historical evidence in the world. So your search-and-rescue mission must be suffused with prayer, good example, and friendship.

The more you rely on prayer, good example, and friendship, the more effective you'll be. The more you pray in particular for the person you want to draw home to the Church, the more efficacious your prayers will be. The more you work at cultivating virtue and setting an unostentatious, joyful, authentic example of Christianity in your own life,[23] the more people will be drawn to ask what the secret of your happiness is.

⌒

Pray

"Do nothing at all unless you begin with prayer," said St. Ephraem the Syrian.[24] Without prayer, even your best

---

[23] Cf. Matt. 5:13-16.

[24] Thigpen, *A Dictionary of Quotes from the Saints,* 171.

search-and-rescue efforts will fail. With prayer, God's grace will supercharge your efforts. (Caution: this doesn't mean you can be lax in your efforts and just assume that God will make up for your laziness. St. Ignatius of Loyola says, "Work as if everything depends on you, and pray as if everything depends on God."[25]) If you pray with faith, you can accomplish seemingly impossible things. As Christ said, "For truly, I say to you, if you have faith as [small as] a grain of mustard seed, you will say to this mountain, 'Move hence to yonder place,' and it will move; and nothing will be impossible to you."[26]

St. Monica, the mother of St. Augustine, knew the power of prayer firsthand. As a young man, her son (whom she had raised a good Catholic) fell away from the Faith, lived a life of debauchery and promiscuity, fathered at least one child out of wedlock, lived illicitly with his girlfriend, and got caught up in a religious cult for several years. Does this sound familiar? Lots of young Catholics are following the same path of sin and dissipation that Augustine traveled when he was young. Their parents are heartsick to see that their children have abandoned the Faith, and they want to know how to bring them home.

[25] St. Ignatius of Loyola (c. 1491-1556), founder of the Jesuit Order.

[26] Matt. 17:20-21.

One of the keys to rescuing them is prayer — relentless, daily petitioning prayer that God will grant them the grace of conversion. If you make prayer a daily priority, as St. Monica did for her wayward son, you'll be amazed at the miracles God can work in the lives of your loved ones (even though you might not see those miracles in this life), even though your loved ones might never know in this life that you were the one praying for their conversion!

God wants to shower the people in your life with graces, and He wants you to become part of the mystery of His generosity by your selfless act of praying for them.[27] Whether you're on a search-and-rescue mission for your son or daughter who has left the Church, a family member, a coworker, or even someone you've only recently met, start and finish your efforts to bring them home with prayer.

Also, keep in mind that you probably won't see any apparent immediate change in the person for whom you're praying. In the mystery of His Providence, God will give him the graces to respond, but whether he accepts them is a secret known only to him and God.

So be patient, and persist in your prayers! Christ used a parable to teach us always to pray and not to lose heart:

[27] Cf. Luke 11:9.

Search and Rescue

"In a certain city there was a judge who neither feared God nor regarded man; and there was a widow in that city who kept coming to him and saying, 'Vindicate me against my adversary.' For a while he refused; but afterward he said to himself, 'Though I neither fear God nor regard man, yet because this widow bothers me, I will vindicate her, or she will wear me out by her continual coming.' " And the Lord said, "Hear what the unrighteous judge says. And will not God vindicate His elect, who cry to Him day and night? Will He delay long over them? I tell you, He will vindicate them speedily."[28]

Your adversary in your search-and-rescue mission isn't the person you seek to rescue. Rather, it's the blindness, the indifference, the hostility, the bad information, the ignorance, the sin, or any of a number of other impediments that block his path home. Those are the adversaries you can vanquish through prayer. In this way, the phrase "search and rescue" takes on a deeper, richer meaning. You're called to rescue your friends and family from imprisonment — imprisonment in sin, in confusion, or in darkness (or in all three).

[28] Luke 18:1-8.

If you doubt the importance and power of prayer in the face of seemingly insurmountable resistance, recall the story of Joshua and the Ark of the Covenant. Joshua and the Israelites were to confront in battle the inhabitants of the fortified city of Jericho. The Israelites were outnumbered, and the defenders of Jericho were protected by high, stout walls that ringed the city. For seven days, the Israelites marched silently around the city walls, praying and bearing in front of them the Ark of the Covenant. You can imagine how puzzled their enemies were at that odd sight. On the seventh day, the Israelites blew their horns in unison, and the walls of the city miraculously crumbled.[29]

You may know someone who seems absolutely unwilling to listen to your message. His fortress of disinterest or hostility toward the Catholic Church may seem, like Jericho, insurmountable. Reaching him may seem impossible. If that's the case, do what Joshua and the Israelites did: Pray!

Set a good example

St. Francis of Assisi said, "Evangelize at all times. When necessary, use words."[30]

---

[29] Cf. Josh. 5-6.
[30] St. Francis of Assisi (c. 1182-1226), founder of the Franciscan Order.

Search and Rescue

This holy man and great apostle of evangelization wasn't being glib. You must take his advice seriously if you want to be effective in your search-and-rescue mission. If you ignore his advice — thinking your words and arguments alone are more important than your personal example — you risk being the ineffectual, useless, clanging gong St. Paul warns about.[31]

Don't underestimate the power and influence your good example can exert on others. Mother Teresa's silent good example evangelized many people and brought them closer to Christ and the Church. Her life of prayer and her love for others were immensely attractive and inspiring. You can inspire others with your own good example. You'll influence and attract others to the Faith if you keep your eyes focused on Christ (the ultimate good example)[32] and live a life of goodness, honesty, joy, and fidelity.

Jesus said, "You are the light of the world. A city set on a hill cannot be hid. Nor do men light a lamp and put it under a bushel, but on a stand, and it gives light to all in the house. Let your light so shine before men, that they may see your good works and give glory to your Father who is in Heaven."[33] Set a good example, and the light of Christ will

[31] Cf. 1 Cor. 13:1.
[32] Cf. Heb. 12:1-2.
[33] Matt. 5:14-16.

radiate from you and draw others to Him. You have Christ's word on it!

⌒

Be a true friend

Don't underestimate the power of friendship in your search-and-rescue mission. You may have made the mistake of entering into discussions about religion with an adversarial attitude — as if you were in a wrestling match. No one wants to be wrestled into saying "uncle" in a discussion about truth. Because we all want to come to see the truth on our own, not be dragged there kicking and screaming, some people put up obstacles to the truth. By being a sincere friend to those you're trying to win for Christ, you can overcome those obstacles.

It's much easier to share the truth with a friend than with a stranger. You already have a level of trust and credibility with your friend. You and your friend enjoy each other's company and have things in common. This can all be put to the service of drawing him closer to Christ and His Church. Because your friend knows and trusts you, you can ask probing (although gentle) questions about his spiritual state, offer advice, and give him evidence that the Catholic Church is the church established by Christ.

Show through your actions and the way you speak — calmly, patiently, and with joy and humor — that you're interested in your friend as a person, not as a potential conquest. Talk candidly about why you're Catholic and why he should be, too. Don't forget that, as a friend, your first duty before God isn't simply to enjoy time with your friend. The deeper meaning and purpose of true friendship is for friends to do what they can to support and help each other get to Heaven. A good friend can exert a strong positive influence through good example and heart-to-heart advice. As Scripture says, "A faithful friend is a sturdy shelter: he that has found one has found a treasure. There is nothing so precious as a faithful friend, and no scales can measure his excellence. A faithful friend is an elixir of life; and those who fear the Lord will find him. Whoever fears the Lord directs his friendship aright, for as he is, so is his neighbor also."[34]

Friendship can include tending to your friend's physical needs as well as his spiritual needs. For many centuries, tending to others' needs — especially through hospitals, clinics, orphanages, food banks, etc. — has been the way that Catholics have begun the process of evangelization. St. James speaks of the necessity of tending to others' needs in search-and-rescue missions: "What does it profit, my brethren, if a

---

[34] Sir. 6:14-17.

man says he has faith but has not works? Can his faith save him? If a brother or sister is ill-clad and in lack of daily food, and one of you says to them, 'Go in peace, be warmed and filled,' without giving them the things needed for the body, what does it profit? So faith by itself, if it has no works, is dead."[35]

One reason Catholic missionaries have been so successful in converting people is their consistent offer of authentic friendship and sincere concern for the well-being of those they serve. Showing genuine concern and giving tangible assistance (when appropriate) for others can likewise be an effective tool in your search-and-rescue mission.

Let your Christian life speak for itself

Prayer, good example, and friendship have more power to move hearts to conversion than all the evidence you can offer. Remember that only God can change hearts, so rely on Him through prayer. But don't stop there. Let your loved ones see for themselves the benefits that come from living according to the Faith — benefits that you're willing to share with them in friendship. These include simple joys such as peace of mind, simplicity, sincerity, and honesty.

[35] James 2:14-17.

Search and Rescue

When your friends see that you're honest, generous, and happy, they'll want to be like you and to be around you. No doubt you gravitate, as I do, to people in your life who are honest, generous, and happy. We all try to avoid greedy, angry liars. That's human nature. So knowing this, heed Christ's words in the Gospel: "Let your light so shine before men, that they may see your good works [as well as your good dispositions] and give glory to your Father who is in Heaven."[36] Your good example as a friend will radiate to those around you, drawing them to want to imitate you (as long as you're sincere, not snooty). Some may secretly desire to be like you and to have the supernatural gifts that you seem to enjoy (such as joy, peace, and an untroubled conscience), but they may never let on that they feel that way. That's fine. Don't worry for a moment about that. Focus instead on making an effort to reach others with Christ's love through your own example. God will take care of what happens after that!

Ask yourself now

• Am I patient and persistent in my prayers when I don't see results?

[36] Matt. 5:16.

• Am I careful to show good example? Do I practice what I preach? Do I show the joy that my Faith brings me so that others will be drawn to live a Christian life?

• When I approach others about the Faith, do I approach them as a friend and show them that I'm concerned for their well-being?

Search-and-rescue action agenda

• Pray the Rosary[37] every day for one month for the conversion of a friend or family member.

• Make a holy hour in front of the Blessed Sacrament once a week and beg Christ to touch that person's heart with graces.[38]

---

[37] The Rosary is a traditional group of prayers consisting of the Apostles' Creed, six Our Fathers, fifty-three Hail Marys, and six Glory Bes, during which you meditate on certain events in the life of Christ and His Blessed Mother. For a step-by-step guide to the Rosary, see *The Essential Rosary*. See also Romano Guardini, *The Rosary of Our Lady*.

[38] A holy hour is time spent in prayer in front of the Blessed Sacrament in response to Christ's invitation to His Apostles to "watch one hour" with Him (cf. Matt. 26:38, 40). Today Christ calls you to keep Him company by spending an occasional hour of prayer in His eucharistic presence. See Benedict Groeschel and James Monti, *In the Presence of Our Lord*.

• Fast from one meal a week as an act of suffering in union with Christ on his behalf.[39] As you fast, meditate on St. Paul's joyful words of prayerful encouragement: "Now I rejoice in my sufferings for your sake, and in my flesh I complete what is lacking in Christ's afflictions for the sake of His Body, that is, the Church."[40]

• Set your watch alarm to beep at noon (or some other time) as a reminder to whisper a short prayer for the one you're hoping to convert.

• Remember St. Paul's exhortation: "First of all, then, I urge that supplications, prayers, intercessions, and thanksgivings be made for all men. . . . This is good, and it is acceptable in the sight of God our Savior, who desires all men to be saved and to come to the knowledge of the truth."[41]

---

[39] Christ invites us all to unite our sufferings with His: "If any man would come after me, let him deny himself and take up his cross and follow me" (Matt. 16:24). Fasting is a form of self-denial that will enable you to accept Christ's invitation. Fasting and prayer can have powerful results (cf. footnote on page 31).

[40] Col. 1:24; cf. Eph. 3:13.

[41] 1 Tim. 2:1, 3-4.

• End your meditations and resolutions with the following prayer:

> Grant, O Lord, that none
> may love Thee less this day
> because of me;
> that never a word or act of mine
> may turn one soul from Thee;
> and, ever daring, yet one more
> grace would I implore:
> that many souls this day,
> because of me,
> may love Thee more.
> Amen.[42]

---

[42] Rev. James D. Watkins, comp., *Manual of Prayers* (Chicago: Midwest Theological Forum, 1998), 70.

Chapter 4

Assess the situation

"My object is . . . to have the naked truth
made known to all who are astray and
to have it revealed by God's help
through my ministry, commending itself so well
that they may embrace and follow it."

St. Augustine

I've given countless seminars throughout the country about Christ and the Catholic Church. In each seminar, I ask the same question:

"How many of you have a family member or a friend who has abandoned the Catholic Church and gone into another religion?" Whether it's fifty people or five thousand, the answer is always the same, always unanimous: everyone in the audience raises a hand.

The fact that you're reading this book suggests that this tragedy has touched your own family and circle of friends, too.

When these Catholics leave the Church, they wander into all sorts of dangers: false doctrine, lukewarmness, secularism and hedonism, and even hatred for the Church. But Christ wants you to help Him help them. He wants you to go out in search of these people and lead them home.

For thus says the Lord God: Behold . . . I myself will search for my sheep, and will seek them out. . . . I will

rescue them from all places where they have been
scattered on a day of clouds and thick darkness. And
I will bring them out from the peoples, and gather
them from the countries, and will bring them into
their own land. . . . I myself will be the shepherd of
my sheep. . . . I will seek the lost, and I will bring back
the strayed, and I will bind up the crippled, and I will
strengthen the weak, and the fat and the strong I will
watch over; I will feed them in justice.[43]

Jesus wants you to help Him find these lost sheep and
bring them back to the fold. Your job is to help reverse this
tide of souls leaving the Church.

But in order to be successful, you first have to find out
why your Aunt Mary and Uncle Jim left the Church and
why your mechanic, Mike, doesn't go to Mass anymore.
Otherwise you may never be able to bring them back to
the Faith.

Finding out why they left could be the hardest part of
your job; often, the reasons people cite aren't the actual
reasons at all. In this chapter, I'll show you some ways to
discern the real reasons they've left the Church and suggest
what you can say and do in response.

[43] Ezek. 34:11-16.

I'll also help you to work with folks who were never Catholic and who resist the idea of becoming Catholic. As in the case with Catholics who leave the Church, moral or doctrinal issues can be stumbling blocks that prevent non-Catholics from becoming Catholic. You can turn those stumbling blocks into stepping-stones if you equip yourself through study and fortify yourself with prayer and the sacraments.[44]

Finally, we'll talk about ways to deal with human tendencies toward laziness, worldliness, and crass self-sufficiency. You've heard it all before: "I don't need any church to tell me how to live my life!" "I'm a good person, and I can live a happy, moral life just as easily on my own, without the Church and all its meddling rules and regulations." These people need you (although they don't realize it yet) to show them why their "I'll do it my way" approach to life won't work.

The more you understand the teachings of the Catholic Church — and the mission of Christ Himself — the more clearly you'll be able to convey to your non-Catholic family and friends why they're being called by Christ to enter into His family: the Church.

[44] See Chapter 5.

Search and Rescue

⌒

Some disagree with Catholic doctrine

Let's turn our attention first to those who leave the Church. Most Catholics who abandon Catholicism embrace other religions, usually becoming Mormons, Jehovah's Witnesses, or Protestants. Catholics like this who migrate to other churches have often told me quite honestly that they left for "doctrinal" reasons. Either they came to reject one or more Catholic teachings, or they didn't feel they were getting "solid preaching" at their parish; and so they went elsewhere in search of it.

Take, for example, your grown son, Rick. You raised him in a good Catholic home, took him to Mass every Sunday, taught him his prayers, drove him to altar-boy practice, and made sure he attended CCD classes. You scrimped and budgeted so you could send him to a Catholic high school. You assumed he'd remain Catholic. Then you found out that in college he became friendly with a large, dynamic group of Evangelical Protestant students who met every week for Bible study.

At first you were happy to see him remaining interested in religious issues, so you didn't give it much thought when he began quoting Bible verses when he came home on weekends. Eventually, you noticed his vocabulary changing.

Phrases such as "The Lord spoke to my heart about this" and "Praise God about that" began to punctuate his speech. Before long, he broke the news to you that he's no longer a Catholic. He left, he explained, because his Evangelical friends convinced him that the Catholic Church is unbiblical and that her traditions are manmade and her doctrines are false.

Rick stopped going to Mass and is now a member of the local "Bible Church" his friends attend. He has become a zealous Protestant, and he does his best to convert you to his way of thinking. Now family get-togethers are tense, often dominated by bitter arguments between your son and other family members over the Catholic Church and her alleged false teachings.

Even though Rick may think he has already discovered the answers in his new church, he still wants, deep down, to grapple with what the Catholic Church claims to be true. Believe it or not, that makes it easier to bring him back to the Church. The techniques explained elsewhere in this book will eventually be very effective with him, because he's concerned with truth, and the Catholic Church is where he can find it.

With people like Rick, never give in to the temptation to lash out in anger or frustration when you don't see them accepting the evidence you offer in support of the Catholic Church. Very often situations like these take a lot of time and careful, steady persistence on your part before they bear fruit. Use the techniques I'm going to teach you in these pages. Be patient, prudent, and charitable, and, with a helpful dose of the facts from Scripture and Church history, you'll be well on your way to bringing Rick, and others like him, home to the Church.

⌒

Some are angry at the Church's
teachings on moral issues

Some people are at odds with the Catholic Church, not because they have a specific theological complaint, but because the Church's teaching on a moral issue interferes with a lifestyle they refuse to abandon. Many such folks are also angry at the Catholic Church (and at Catholics); their anger protects them from having to confront the Church's teachings on issues they find painful, such as contraception, homosexuality, abortion, and divorce.

For example, in our era, untold millions of women and men have been traumatized by the sin of abortion. They are the "walking wounded" of our society, souls who appear happy and intact outwardly, but who suffer unspeakable anguish and remorse in the silence of their hearts.

Rather than repenting of their sin and returning to the peace and forgiveness that God wants so much to extend, some women who have had abortions fall into prideful stubbornness, directing their anger at the Church or at God Himself. Their anger can turn into irrational rage, as I discovered a few years ago.

I was on a plane from San Diego to New York. Sitting next to me was a pleasant, middle-aged woman on her way to Europe for a vacation with her husband (he was already there, wrapping up a business trip). She and I exchanged pleasantries, and before long the conversation moved into more personal areas. She told me about her family, her two children in college, and her own career. She also mentioned that she was Catholic, although she remarked snidely that she had no use for this Pope and that she hoped for "progress" in the Church's teachings once the "old guy" was out of the way. That was my first clue that there was a problem.

When she asked me about myself, I pulled out a picture of my family and handed it to her, telling her that I was married with eight children.[45] That's where the conversation took a sharp turn for the worse.

[45] At the time we had eight children. Now, thanks be to God, we have eleven.

Her eyes widened when I said "eight children." From her horrified look, I might as well have said, "Here, hold this rattlesnake."

She blinked, her mouth slightly open. "You have eight children?"

"Yes, and my wife and I would love to . . ."

"How . . ." she sputtered, interrupting me with a spasm of flustered astonishment. "Why would you have so many children?" she demanded. Anger flashed in her face, swiftly replacing her astonishment. For the next few moments she stared acidly as I tried unsuccessfully to explain why my wife and I believe in being open to life.

The more I talked, the angrier she got. Waving her finger in my face, she told me how she hated the Catholic Church for saying abortion was wrong. She herself had had three abortions, the first while she was a college coed, when a date rape resulted in pregnancy. A few years later, her boyfriend forced her to abort two more children.

It was clear to me that, in each case, her hatred for the men involved fed her anguish and distorted her view of God, the Church, and herself. As she had been victimized by the men who caused her to have three abortions, so, she reasoned, my wife had been "victimized" by me, and that was something I should be ashamed of.

As she spoke, her finger stabbing the air in front of my face for emphasis, I could see the burning pain in her eyes. Her white-hot anger at men and at the Church — at me! — was a self-defense against the truth of what she had done. Our conversation ended on that abrupt and awkward note.

Since that day, I have prayed for her often, asking God to give her the grace and courage to walk out of her prison of pain and remorse over what she had done. I knew that, in that situation, there was nothing I could say or do to reach her directly, but I was able to pray for her.

You, too, know people who have been wounded by some past sin or negative experience. Start by praying for them, and do what you can, as gently and patiently as possible, to speak to them about Christ's loving forgiveness. Remind them, if you can, that He loves them and will forgive anything, no matter how bad they think it may be, if they approach him with a contrite heart. Later we'll discuss some things I've learned that can be helpful in such difficult circumstances.

⌒

Some have no interest in religion at all

Apathy — rather than disagreement with the Church's theological or moral teachings — keeps other people out of the Church or causes Catholics to stop attending Mass.

Search and Rescue

These people don't attend any church; they're not concerned with moral or doctrinal issues; they don't care about religion at all. These souls drift down the lazy current of modern, me-centered secularism and technology-worship, into spiritual oblivion. They're not concerned with truth and error; they just want to satisfy their appetites. Computers, entertainment, the Stock Market, consumerism, sports, the Internet, alcohol, illicit sex, gambling, or other empty sensual pursuits are their religion.

Take your Uncle Joe as an example. He divorced his wife, bought a Corvette, and is now living with a woman twenty years younger than he. Uncle Joe no longer goes to Mass. He hasn't been to Confession in years. He pays his alimony, sees his kids every other weekend, and enjoys having friends over on Sundays for beer and watching the ball game on his expensive home entertainment system. Although outwardly he seems to be a pretty decent fellow, inwardly he's a moral slob. He's not at all likely to be swayed by appeals to the Bible or the Church Fathers. You have to approach Uncle Joe differently.

His slide out of the Church began when he ceased praying every day. It accelerated when he stopped going to Mass and Confession. He grew hardened and unrepentant in his vices. It wasn't a barrage of non-Catholic arguments that jostled him loose from his Catholic moorings. It was his unchecked appetites and love of pleasure: like hidden termites, these vices slowly but inevitably undermined the structure of his Catholic faith, which then collapsed. All that was left standing was his own desire to do what he wanted.

Later we'll consider how to approach amoral people like your Uncle Joe. For now, it's enough to say that, like the angry woman on the plane, he can't be won over by Scripture, because he's just not interested. As we'll see, there are ways to help him, though.

⌒

Some are scandalized by some Catholics' bad example

"Eric" left the Catholic Church several years ago because he decided to live an active homosexual life. At the time he left, he was married to a loving wife with whom he had several happy, healthy children. He had a good job, a promising career, and, by all outward appearances, an ideal personal situation. He gave those things up, along with his Catholic Faith, when he stepped out of the security and stability of marriage and family into the chaos of the promiscuous homosexual subculture. Although he had always felt a certain same-sex attraction, Eric had fought those temptations and largely conquered them. A happy marriage and the demands of raising a family kept him busy with the normal duties of a husband and father. But then something happened that destabilized him.

Eric is a member of my family, and I know that in his case, his rejection of the Catholic Church wasn't like that of Uncle Joe, who slowly gave in to his sinful impulses (although that, ultimately, was a factor for Eric, too). A major reason for Eric's fall away from the Faith was that he had been repeatedly "propositioned" by a Catholic priest who himself secretly lived an active homosexual life. Eventually, the priest weakened Eric's resolve. "If even a 'good' priest could be so willing to do this," Eric later confided in me, "why should I say no to it?" Scandal weakened him in the face of temptation and allowed him to be engulfed by it.

From Eric's erroneous but powerful conclusion — "If he's doing it, why can't I?" — it was a short, effortless step for Eric to accept the invitation the next time it was offered. From then on, Eric's view of the Church, of truth, and of himself was warped, rendering him nearly incapable of looking at the clergy without deep suspicion about their true motives.

You know people who have suffered such wounds. They may not have been scandalized by the things that scandalized Eric — there are many things that can cause scandal by Catholics, not just sexual misbehavior — but they were injured by similar scandals.

Your family or friends who left the Church may be reluctant to tell you about something similar that overthrew them. They may offer you a variety of other, secondary, reasons for their departure. But if you listen carefully, you may be able to discern their real reasons.

Scandal given by Catholics, especially those in authority, causes many people to leave the Church and can leave deep wounds that keep those who leave from coming home. It can likewise prevent non-Catholics from ever entering the Church. "Catholics are hypocrites," they think. "They say one thing and do another." Although this is true of some Catholics, it's not true of all; and it's not true of the Church herself. The Church is holy even though some or even many of her members may be anything but holy.

Although Catholics cause damage by their bad example, that damage can be repaired. Here again, it isn't a doctrinal or scriptural task you have ahead of you; no, you've got to rely on indirect personal approaches. In such cases, as we'll see later, your search-and-rescue mission will have to depend, first and foremost, on the honesty and genuineness of your own life. By your own example, you'll have to begin by convincing them that, in spite of the behavior of some Catholics, the Catholic Church is still the church established by Christ, guarded and guided by the Holy Spirit.

Search and Rescue

⌒

*Some are angry because they think
the Church abandoned them*

Another type of scandal, one that has wounded and antagonized many older Catholics, is the scandal of heterodoxy and disrespect for the Holy Sacrifice of the Mass.[46] This became a widespread problem as the Church was transformed by Vatican II[47] while American society, in particular, suffered several major upheavals: the "sexual revolution," the Vietnam War, and the dizzying rise of technology. Many Catholics grew angry at changes in the way Mass was celebrated and at the unorthodox ideas and attitudes adopted by many priests, nuns, and laypeople. They felt the Church had abandoned them, and many, in sullen resentment, left the Church: "I didn't leave the Church; the Church left me."

These Catholics can be brought home. Their concerns and angers are rooted in a deep love and reverence for Tradition and the Mass, although the ways in which they tried to solve or combat the problems they saw were often wrong. Martin Luther, for example, saw a deep need for reform in

---

[46] Heterodoxy is the departure from orthodox teaching and practice; the embracing of erroneous or defective teaching and practice.

[47] 1962-1965.

the Catholic Church in the sixteenth century, but he chose the wrong path to try to deal with the problem: He left the Church and started the Protestant Reformation, which was in reality not a reformation, but a rebellion. And his act has led countless souls into confusion, error, doctrinal division, and fragmentation.[48] St. Francis of Assisi, on the other hand, also saw deep problems in the Church of his day that urgently needed reform. He, unlike Luther, chose the right path: he remained in the Church and followed God's direction to help clean things up. He remained a faithful son of the Church, and thus God could use him to help reform the abuses and problems that had sprung up in the Church.

⌒

Some are angry with God

You may encounter in some people a bitterness toward God. Because of the death of a child or a spouse, a financial setback, a divorce, or some other personal catastrophe, many people become angry at God: "Why did You let this happen to me, God?" they cry out defiantly. For many, this emotional estrangement prevents them from seeing past the tragedy and seeing that God does love them and wants to draw them

---

[48] For an account of these problems, and the specific issues Catholics can focus on to help Protestants come home to the Church, see my book *Surprised by Truth 2*.

home. Keep this in mind prayerfully when you speak with your family and friends, because in spite of your biblical arguments, their anger toward God may block them from seeing the Church objectively. In these cases, prayer and fasting for that person, combined with patience and great kindness from you, are more powerful than your arguments alone.

☛

What keeps non-Catholics from
coming into the Church?

Recall the last time you saw news coverage of a devastating hurricane, earthquake, or tornado. First on the scene, once the disaster passed, were the rescue workers and clean-up crews. While paramedics cared for the wounded, bull-dozers and tow trucks fanned out to remove debris from the roads. All the fallen trees, wrecked cars, twisted metal from destroyed buildings, downed power lines, rubble — all of it — had to be cleared away before life could get back to normal.

As a search-and-rescue apostle, you must do similar work when you seek to bring non-Catholics home to the Church. Think of yourself as a tool God can use to clear away the intellectual or emotional rubble that blocks another person from being able to see and embrace the Catholic Faith. This is true, of course, in the case of former Catholics, too, but even more so in the case of those who have never been Catholic.

There are several reasons why non-Catholics stay away from the Church.

~

Some have misconceptions about the Catholic Church

Many non-Catholics labor under a host of misconceptions about what the Catholic Church is and teaches. I know, because not only do I run into these misconceptions among non-Catholics I meet, but I've been to many Protestant worship services and have heard ministers thunder from the pulpit about Catholics being "idol worshipers," "Mary worshipers," "opposed to the Bible," and "trying to earn their salvation." I'm sure you've encountered these and other kinds of misconceptions about Catholics. Your non-Catholic friend has inherited many of them; as a search-and-rescue apostle, you've got to remove this debris of error so that, once the path is cleared, his heart and mind can move forward toward the truth.[49]

----

[49] The following books will help you clear up misconceptions non-Catholics have about Mary, the Pope, the Mass, and Tradition and the Bible: *Catholicism and Fundamentalism, Surprised by Truth 2, Where Is That in the Bible?, Pope Fiction: Answers to 30 Myths and Misconceptions About the Papacy, Catholic for a Reason,* vols. 1 and 2, and *Hail Holy Queen.*

Search and Rescue

⤦

Some have prejudices against the Catholic Church

Cultural and religious prejudice against the Catholic
Church prevents many non-Catholics from entering the
Church. These deeply ingrained prejudices tend to be
handed down in family and social settings or are learned
from the media. Television and movies, for example, churn
out plenty of fresh anti-Catholic bias on a daily basis.[50] It's
no wonder, then, that some of your non-Catholic family and
friends dislike the Catholic Church: they've been condi-
tioned to see the Church as sinister, hypocritical, kooky, or
all three. From a religious standpoint, there's also the deep
Protestant anti-Catholic bias that has permeated many levels of American society for over two hundred years. This entrenched prejudice is hard to overcome, but God's grace and
your own good example and command of the facts will be
potent antidotes to the virulent bias you'll sometimes
encounter in your non-Catholic friends.[51]

---

[50] For details on this sad fact, see the Catholic League's
"Annual Report on Anti-Catholicism."

[51] A good place to start in overcoming prejudice against
the Church is to give your friend a copy of my book
Surprised by Truth 2, a collection of conversion stories
of former non-Catholics, from Protestant, Mormon,
secular, atheistic, and other backgrounds.

There's also the simple hatred of Catholics because of the moral stand the Church takes on issues such as abortion and contraception. "Pro-choice" extremists are masters at whipping up prejudices against the Pope, the Catholic Church, and faithful Catholics by accusing them of being "intolerant" for wanting to protect unborn children from abortion.[52]

In the face of prejudices, your task in your search-and-rescue mission is threefold:

• *First, equip yourself with the basic facts you need to counteract them.*[53]

• *Second, keep calm, don't get angry, and realize that Christ is allowing you to help Him liberate that person from his prison of prejudice.* It might take time to accomplish, but if you remain patient and charitable in the face of ridicule and suspicion, your chances of rescuing that person are excellent. Remember that many people were

---

[52] Two Catholic organizations that can provide you with the facts and information you need to discuss and defend the Church's teachings on contraception and abortion are Human Life International and One More Soul.

[53] In Chapter 5, we'll discuss how to prepare yourself for your search-and-rescue mission. See also the reading plan at the end of this book.

taught these prejudices by others, and such lessons, once learned, can be hard to "unlearn." So be patient.

• *Finally, pray for the graces you and your non-Catholic friend need.* Christ wants to fortify your natural abilities with his grace — ask Him for His help, and He'll give it to you!

Some have genuine disagreements with the Church

Another reason non-Catholics reject the Church stems from some specific objections to Catholic teachings. In the case of Protestants, Mormons, and Jehovah's Witnesses, there tend to be Bible-based objections. Clearly, there may also be prejudice and misconceptions that lurk in the background, but that isn't so with all non-Catholics. Many are sincere, open, and very intelligent. They simply disagree with Catholic teachings and have biblical and historical reasons for pressing their objection. Here again, you must prepare yourself to explain Catholic teaching intelligently, defend it charitably, and share it effectively.[54] Don't try to "wing it" when it comes to these situations. You need to do your homework, get the facts and give a solid answer to their questions — if

[54] See Chapter 5.

you don't, the non-Catholic may wrongly assume that because you didn't have a good answer to his objection (or couldn't get back to him with one) that no good Catholic response exists. You may not have a ready reply to a given question or objection, but the answers are available. You'll simply need to go get them and then come back with the information that will help your friend.

Genuine disagreements can be resolved, but it will take effort on your part to gather the answers to their questions, coupled with a strong spirit of humble charity. Remember what St. Ignatius of Loyola advised: "Work as if everything depends on you, and pray as if everything depends on God." If you follow this simple wisdom, you'll make great headway with your non-Catholic family and friends.

⌒

Some suffer from the "I'm Not Being Fed" syndrome

You'll also run into what I call the "I'm Not Being Fed" syndrome. You know people who suffer from this. Many non-Catholics and former Catholics do. They say things such as "The Mass is boring," "I don't get anything out of the Catholic Church," and, "I went to the local Bible church because I just wasn't being fed at the Catholic Church."

It's true that many Catholic parishes *are* boring, but that's irrelevant. Some priests give lackluster sermons at best. Other parishes have lively preaching, but the people in the pews seem cold and disinterested in newcomers. On the other hand, some Catholic parishes have lively preaching and a vibrant community, but some tend not to preach the hard truths of the Faith, and you sense there a general theological malaise in areas of objective truth. You've probably visited parishes like this. Regardless of how well or poorly the priest preaches, regardless of how good or lame the music is, regardless of how many people smile at you or glad-hand you after Mass, none of these things touches on the issue of whether the Catholic Church is the one true Church established by Christ.[55]

The Mass isn't entertainment. It is worship of the Blessed Trinity in spirit and in truth.[56] Your formation as a search-and-rescue apostle will help restore vibrancy to your parish while enabling you to show others that vibrancy isn't the criterion by which to choose a church; truth is, Christ's truth. And that is found fully only in the Catholic Church.

☞

Some hide their reasons for leaving

We've talked about people who are willing to give you their reasons for not entering the Church or for leaving it:

---

[55] Cf. Matthew 16:18-19.
[56] Cf. John 4:23.

your son Rick, who joined a Bible church; the woman on the plane, who vociferously objected to the Church's teaching on abortion; Uncle Joe, who's living openly in immorality, and even Eric, who's willing (at least privately) to point out the scandal that drove him out of the Church. In each of these cases, before you make further progress, you'll have to address the issues that trouble these people. Don't give up: the fact that they don't hide their reasons means that you have a good chance to help them.

It's far more difficult when people won't tell you the real reason they left the Church. In these cases, you need to use patience and sensitivity to discern why they left so that you can discover the best way to help bring them home.

Your cousin Amy is a good example. Recently, she and her husband, Ron, broke the news that they're no longer in the Catholic Church. Amy told you that she and Ron weren't "getting anything out of" their local parish, so they switched to a more vibrant Christian community — a Calvary Chapel church. You were heartbroken and bewildered. Unless you listen carefully, patiently, and sensitively, you may never discover that the reason she gave you wasn't the real reason for their leaving. The real reason was artificial contraception.

Amy grew up Catholic and went to a Catholic high school and college. When she married at age twenty-three, she and her husband didn't want to start a family right away, so even though they were married in the Catholic Church, they agreed that she would go on the pill. They had been given erroneous advice from other Catholics, including a priest, who told them it was fine to use artificial contraceptives as long as their conscience told them it was OK. "It's between you and God," their friends assured them.

Their break with the Church occurred when a new pastor was assigned to their parish. In his sermon one Sunday, this dynamic young priest explained in clear, unequivocal terms the Church's teaching that artificial contraception is wrong.

This made Amy mad.

She was on the pill because she and her husband weren't ready for kids yet. They wanted to save enough money and furnish their new home before they started having the burden and expense of children.

After Mass, she confronted the young priest and asked him to explain what he meant by saying that the Church forbids artificial contraception. He explained, gently but firmly, and she grew even angrier. This meant that she and her husband would have to change their lifestyle — a lifestyle they had become accustomed to. Their comfortable dual income and upscale lifestyle would be disrupted if she were to get pregnant.

Within a few weeks, Amy and her husband left that parish and, knowing that they'd be likely to run into this unpleasant message at other Catholic churches, began attending the nearby Calvary Chapel. Their transition to the world of Protestantism was a bit difficult, but Amy and her husband soon felt comfortable in a community where the music was lively and contraception was considered no big deal: most of the married couples in that church, including the young pastor and his wife, used contraceptives.

Amy left the Catholic Church, not because she disagreed with some biblical teaching, but because she didn't want to change her lifestyle. She had become accustomed to using contraception, and regardless of what the Church said, she wasn't going to stop. But she didn't want to admit this to you.

In many instances, men and women struggle with a moral teaching such as this that they're not yet willing to accept, but, rather than admit that, even to themselves, they blame the Church for being boring or unbiblical or some other thing.

If your loved ones offer an unsubstantial reason for leaving the Church, and you sense in them a deeper issue with the Church, first gently and tactfully make an effort to draw out their real reason for leaving the Church. This often takes time and patience, but if you're careful and sensitive, you can probably find out what it is.

If you don't proceed here patiently and sensitively, you'll waste a lot of time discussing the wrong topics. But if you first listen sympathetically, they may soon reveal to you that they've left the Church because they disagree with one of her moral teachings (and not because Mass is boring). Then you'll know where to begin your search-and-rescue mission.

I know many couples who left the Catholic Church over a moral issue such as sterilization and contraception, but returned when they were shown why these practices are wrong. Your task, in such cases, will be to come to an understanding of the Church's teachings on these issues and learn to explain them to those who disagree. Learn first to listen in such cases and then how to talk with others about the life-giving truth of Catholic moral teaching and how openness to life brings happiness and liberation to marriage. This can be the catalyst of grace to bring them home.

☞

Listen to what they're not saying

Remember that friendship is a critical element in your search-and-rescue mission. Friendship requires careful listening: you must learn how to listen to your family and friends with your heart as much as, or more than, with your ears.

Listen to what each of them is *not* saying, and you'll discern, often at very deep, hidden levels of the heart, the needs of that soul, and how you can help him or her.

There's no formula or technique for this. Each of us is different and will be able to do this with greater or lesser levels of skill, but you can begin now to pray for God's grace to illuminate your mind so you'll see more deeply into the person you're trying to help in your search-and-rescue mission. Whether it's your relative who has left the Church, a non-Catholic friend who holds misconceptions about Catholicism or has antagonism toward it, or even someone who hates God and religion altogether, you have it in your power, by God's grace, to listen and look for those deeper, unspoken issues that often lie behind a person's arguments against the Faith.

Listen carefully when a former Catholic or non-Catholic argues against the Church; look for clues about some inner pain or anger lurking beneath the veneer of those arguments. Often, that deeper issue is what needs to be addressed and resolved before any progress can be made in the area of biblical or historical objections.

I'm sure you know people who carry around inside them like lead weights the burdens of deep, unresolved negative issues and emotions. Most likely, you know people in your family or circle of friends who churn inside with anger or suspicion, with long-held grudges they simply can't or won't let go of, with resentments born of real or perceived slights, or with feelings of envy or irritation that cloud and weaken their ability to consider the Church objectively. Many people live hidden lives of pain from past sins that still cause them intense guilt and anguish. For many people, abortion, murder, theft, adultery, and other past sins are specters of self-accusation and remorse that have never been exorcised because these souls haven't repented of those sins or gone to Confession.

Listen with your heart

The key is to begin listening with your heart; listen for those subtle undercurrents that may run swiftly but far out of sight in your friend's heart. You're not a mind-reader, of course. God knows that, and He doesn't expect you suddenly to have the ability to peer into the hidden recesses of the human heart. Rather, He wants you to get into the habit of looking for clues that can help you help others come home.

Pray often for the grace to listen with your heart as well as with your ears, and be open to the promptings of the Holy Spirit as He seeks to use you as His instrument in the world.

Of course, it's important to remember that not everybody is masking deep emotional problems or guilt beneath their objections to the Catholic Church. Many non-Catholics and ex-Catholics simply have honest, heartfelt objections, and you have to keep that in mind. Look for clues that may help you listen at deeper levels, but don't make the mistake of assuming that everything is a mask for a personal problem. Sometimes an objection is simply that: an objection. Always be ready to respond to objections with the same kind of firm but friendly, charitable approach. Remember the words of St. Paul to Timothy:

And the Lord's servant must not be quarrelsome but kindly to everyone, an apt teacher, forbearing, correcting his opponents with gentleness. God will perhaps grant that they will repent and come to know the truth.[57]

Let God's grace show you how to respond to unspoken issues

There's a remarkable story about the late Archbishop Fulton Sheen that illustrates what a master he was at

[57] 2 Tim. 2:24-26.

listening with his heart. Before giving a talk at a parish one evening, he was dining in the rectory with the pastor and a young associate parish priest. The young priest strongly criticized the Catholic Church for her wealth, prodding Archbishop Sheen with pointed questions about why the Vatican didn't sell its holdings and valuables and give the money to the poor. Sheen gave the standard explanation, but that didn't satisfy this priest.[58] He continued badgering the archbishop, scoffing at the Church's "opulence." After a few frustrating attempts to answer the argumentative priest's challenges, Sheen took the priest aside out of earshot of the others.

The archbishop fixed the younger man with a steely gaze. "Father, how long have you been stealing from the collection basket?"

The look on the young priest's face said it all, and his story tumbled out. He had been skimming money from the parish collection basket for some time, and his wrath against the Church's "wealth" was the pressure-release valve for his soul, a way he could relieve some of the accumulating pain and anxiety of his guilty conscience. Rather than stop his

---

[58] The response to this argument is found in my book *Pope Fiction* (San Diego: Basilica Press, 1999), 116-118.

sinful activity, repent, and go to Confession, he chose the path of haranguing the Church for being too "wealthy."

Imagine the power of God's grace working in that priest's soul at that moment, all because Archbishop Sheen listened with his heart, and not just with his ears. How was Sheen able to discern this deep issue lurking below the surface of the arguments? Only God's grace can account for it. But that grace isn't reserved for bishops. It's available to you, in the measure God knows is right and appropriate for you, if you simply begin asking Him to give it to you.

But don't fall into the trap of trying to psychoanalyze everyone around you and become suspicious that every non-Catholic you encounter is harboring some dark secret. This chapter isn't intended to suggest that you should assume hidden motives are at work in all cases — just that they may be at work in some cases. Learning to spot them when they come up takes practice, prayer, and the gift of God's grace of discernment and illumination.

One of my friends, who's a doctor, used to work at prolife information booths on college campuses in the '70s and '80s. He told me about his experiences in talking with students, many of whom attacked and berated him vociferously for daring to promote the prolife cause on college campuses (typically, bastions of pro-abortion rhetoric and activism).

Search and Rescue

His experiences in learning how to deal with different people in different ways can help you in your search-and-rescue mission. He told me how, when young men would come up and badger him, he'd recognize that they were simply spouting the stupid arguments drummed into them by radical feminist professors and the ubiquitous pro-abortion propaganda on college campuses. He'd respond to their arguments with a vigorous dose of common sense and medical facts. Sometimes, students would show genuine interest in learning more about the case for protecting unborn life.

There were other instances, however, when he would suddenly be faced with a shouting, raging female student who seemed to have become unhinged by the presence of the pro-life booth and by his arguments claiming that a fetus is not just a blob of tissue, but is in fact a tiny, living human baby. This irrational rage couldn't have been brought about by the arguments for and against abortion. Its cause had to be deeper: these young women were almost always suffering from the deep, self-inflicted wounds of abortions. In these cases, since their anger was so out of proportion to the situation, my friend knew that he had to listen with his heart. He knew that what these women needed at that moment was not a barrage of facts and figures about how terrible abortion is. They needed kindness and compassion; they needed to be encouraged gently to heal this pain by turning to Christ and the sacrament of Confession. Many of these young women were able to come home to Christ and to the sacraments as a result of my friend's astute habit of listening carefully.[59] He modeled well Christ's reaction to the woman caught in adultery[60] — offering gentle compassion, accompanied by firm encouragement to strive after virtue.

In your search-and-rescue missions, follow his example and Fulton Sheen's. You'll be much more effective in helping your friends and family. Be ready, willing, and able to give reasons for your Catholic beliefs and answers to the objections people raise against them,[61] but first be attentive and compassionate.

Never forget that as human beings, we're all prone to being influenced by our emotions. Often our judgment can be clouded by guilt and feelings of anger or resentment. When these feelings stem from bad experiences people have had with Catholics, they complicate the process of helping that person overcome his objections to the Church.

---

[59] Two powerful examples in the life of Christ show Him revealing a deeper problem in someone's life: the case of the rich young man (Matt. 19:16-26; Mark 10:17-22) and the case of the Samaritan woman at the well (John 4:4-26).

[60] John 8:1-11.

[61] Cf. Jude 3; 1 Pet. 3:15.

Search and Rescue

Again, God doesn't expect you to become a mind-reader. What He does ask is that you rely on His grace to guide you and do your best to listen and respond to what others say and to what they *don't* say.

Ask yourself now

• Have I accepted Christ's call to help Him bring souls into the Catholic Church?

• Do I know what's keeping my loved ones away from Christ or from the Catholic Church?

• Do I listen to them with my heart so that I may discern the best way to approach them about the Faith?

Search-and-rescue action agenda

• Pray for the grace of illumination so you'll be able to discern unspoken issues that lie beneath the surface of arguments or complaints about the Church.

• Listen attentively. Really listen and consider the merits of the other person's point. Don't be so busy thinking up your own response that you miss what the other person is really saying. It's easy to look as if you're listening, when in fact you're just waiting for the other person to stop talking so you can skewer his argument. Don't listen that way.

• Let your listener know that you're paying attention. Nod your head to show understanding if not agreement. Smile when appropriate, or at least don't scowl or look defensive. Occasionally repeat key elements of the other person's argument to show you understand it.

• End your resolutions with the following prayer:

Come, Holy Spirit!
Holy Spirit, Lord of light,
from the clear celestial heights,
Thy pure beaming radiance give.
Come, Thou Father of the poor,
come with treasures which endure;
Come, Thou Light of all that live.
Light immortal, Light divine,
visit Thou these hearts of Thine.
And our inmost being fill.
If Thou take Thy grace away,
nothing pure in man will stay.
All his good is turned to ill.

Search and Rescue

Heal our wounds, our strength renew;
On our dryness pour Thy dew.
Wash the stains of guilt away.
Bend the stubborn heart and will;
Melt the frozen, warm the chill;
Guide the steps that go astray.
Amen.[62]

---

[62] Attributed to Pope Innocent III (1160-1216); translated by Edward Caswall, 1814-1878; stanzas 1, 3, and 4.

Chapter 5

Prepare yourself

"Learning unsupported by grace may get
into our ears; it never reaches the heart. But
when God's grace touches our innermost minds
to bring understanding, His word that has been
received by the ear sinks deep into the heart."

St. Isidore of Seville

Listening with your heart is essential to your success as a search-and-rescue apostle, but it isn't enough. Once your careful listening has enabled you to discern the real issues that are keeping your cousin Linda or your friend Scott outside the Church, you have to know how to address those issues so that Linda and Scott will be able to understand and accept what the Church teaches. To be able to do that, you must do some homework and learn some basic skills. You can't give what you don't have. You may be fired up about sharing the Faith with others. You may have learned to listen and may be ready and willing to speak to those around you. But unless you prepare yourself with knowledge of the Faith, your enthusiasm and goodwill won't get you anywhere.

Worse, without a solid understanding of the Faith, you risk misinforming people and even making it harder for non-Catholics to embrace Christ and His Church.

I remember a conversation I heard a few years ago between a Catholic and an Evangelical Protestant. It took place during the intermission at a parish apologetics seminar I was conducting. A crowd of Catholics were milling around the book tables at the back of the auditorium. In their midst was a young man in his mid-twenties, bubbling over with newfound enthusiasm for apologetics. I watched as he animatedly explained something to another man. As I drew closer, I began to hear what they were saying and realized that although the young Catholic was admirably enthusiastic in the way he presented his arguments, he was terribly unprepared for the task. They were discussing the Catholic doctrine of the Immaculate Conception, and it was obvious that although the young man believed fervently in the doctrine, he didn't have a clue about how to defend it. A small crowd of Catholics were standing by, listening closely to the discussion.

The young man was arguing that since Mary is the one from who Christ received His human nature, she had to have been immaculately conceived and kept free from sin; otherwise she would have passed on to her Son a sinful human nature.

Without missing a beat, the Protestant replied, "If your argument is correct, then Mary's parents and her grandparents on both sides also must also have been sinless, and so on, stretching back to the time of Adam and Eve. Do you really expect me to believe that Mary's entire family tree was immaculately conceived?"

I had to step in.

I agreed with the Protestant that the young Catholic's arguments were not convincing, but I pointed out that they're also not the reasons the Church claims that Mary was immaculately conceived. [63]

This episode of an exuberant but unprepared Catholic was very instructive for me (and, I hope, for him, too). It showed me just how important it is to be prepared. The situation could have led people into error. For example, after refuting the young Catholic's false argument, the Protestant could have gone on to deliver a five-minute, Bible-based argument intended to show that the doctrine of Mary's Immaculate Conception is unbiblical. He would have been wrong, but he would have had greater credibility with the Catholics who were listening primarily because he had just clearly shown the falsity of one argument the young Catholic was using.

[63] For a good explanation of the Immaculate Conception and how to explain it to non-Catholics (especially to Protestants), see Leon J. Suprenant, Jr., Scott Hahn, et al., *Catholic for a Reason: Scripture and the Mystery of the Mother of God*, and Father Mateo, *Refuting the Attack on Mary*. For other books that explain Catholic doctrines, see the reading plan at the end of this book.

Search and Rescue

That would have fostered a measure of skepticism among some of the Catholics. "If that Catholic guy was wrong about that point," they might have reasoned to themselves, "what else was he wrong about?"

And of the Protestant, some might have mused, "He was right about that point. I wonder what else he's right about. And if he's right about other things, then it's likely the Catholic Church is wrong." You can see how lack of preparation can, in some cases, actually do harm.

☞

Proclaim what the Church teaches — no less, no more

Lack of study can also harm your own faith. If you don't educate yourself on Church teachings and practices, you can fall into the classic trap of proclaiming what the Church doesn't teach.

In the early 1990s, a colleague and I were conducting an apologetics seminar at a large parish in Los Angeles. During the question-and-answer segment, my colleague answered a question on salvation outside the Church, and a scruffy young man in horn-rimmed glasses stood up, strode down the center aisle, and began smacking his shoes together loudly.

"Heresy!" he shouted. "What you just said is heresy!" he bellowed, clapping his shoes vigorously.

Nobody moved. The speaker stopped in mid-sentence. The pastor of the parish sat with his mouth open, with an unspoken question in his expression: "Who's *this* nut?" — exactly what all of us were wondering at that moment.

The young man, seeing he had everyone's attention, stopped the shoe-clapping for a moment. He glanced around at the shocked faces, then turned and barked at the speaker again: "You're teaching heresy! This so-called Pope is a heretic for saying that non-Catholics can be saved! He's not a valid pope. And you're a heretic for teaching his error! All of you are being deceived!"

With that he gave another couple of claps, grabbed his knapsack, and headed toward the rear of the church, all the while continuing his high-decibel mantra of "Heresy! Heresy!" The walls reverberated with the echoes of his outburst as he pushed through the front doors and disappeared.

Judging from the leaflets he had left lying in the pews, this angry young man seemed to have been a member of a Catholic group that is at odds with what the Church teaches on the question of salvation outside the Church.[64] There are

[64] For an explanation of the background and parties to this controversy of the Catholic dogma of *extra ecclesiam nulla salus* ("outside the Church there is no salvation"), including the explication of this doctrine according to Vatican II, and in light of the teachings of past councils,

many splinter groups associated with the Church, some more vehement than others in their attacks on the Church's teaching, but all of them united in their opposition to the validity of the Second Vatican Council and to the *Catechism*.

A few minutes after that man had stormed out of the church, it dawned on me what he was doing with his shoes. He must have believed he was following Christ's injunction to His disciples to "shake the dust off [their] feet"[65] as a reproach to those who refused to listen to the gospel of repentance and salvation. It was this young man's colorful way of letting us know that *he* had the true Catholic Faith, not we, and certainly not the Pope.

That man believed, as members of such groups invariably do, that he knew better than the Pope and the bishops what constitutes Catholic doctrine. In fact, this fellow had become his own Pope. By rejecting the lawful teaching authority of the Catholic Church — the Pope and the college of bishops, teaching in union with the Pope — in favor of his own particular understanding of doctrine, he had in effect become no less a Protestant than was Luther.

popes, and Fathers of the Church, see Francis Sullivan, S.J., *Salvation Outside the Church?* See also Pope Pius XII, *Mystici Corporis Christi*.

[65] Cf. Mark 6:11; Luke 10:10-12.

This agitated man who disrupted our seminar was doing more than merely harming his own spiritual state by his angry rejection of the Pope and the Church's teaching authority. He was also scandalizing those attending the conference, especially the non-Catholics. This is a particular danger you must guard against. If you're not vigilant, it can creep into and undermine your own efforts to explain and defend the Catholic Faith.

Ubi Petrus, ibi ecclesia: "Where Peter is, there is the Church." The meaning of this Latin maxim is clear: if we're with Peter and his successors, the popes, we're with the Church. To be effective in your search-and-rescue missions to friends, family members, and strangers, you have to be sure you share *authentic* Catholicism, not some variant of it. You mustn't leave out elements of the Faith, nor can you add things that don't belong. You're called by Christ to "contend for the Faith which was once for all delivered to the saints."[66] Anything other than that Faith is defective and will harm those you pass it on to.

How can you be sure you're "with" the Pope and that you stand for authentic Catholicism? The simplest way is to ask yourself three questions:

[66] Jude 3.

Search and Rescue

• *Have I made an effort to ensure that I am familiar with the basic teachings of the Catholic Church as set forth in the* Catechism?

You can't believe in something you are ignorant of. So when it comes to the doctrines of the Catholic Faith, you have to make the effort to know what they are so that you can believe in them.

• *Do I willfully reject one or more teachings of the Catholic Church?*

To be with the Church, you must embrace her teachings, even the hard ones that may require you to change the way you live. You mustn't disregard the Church's teachings on moral issues or reject any doctrine, such as Purgatory or the reality of personal sin and the need for repentance and reconciliation.

• *Do I willingly assent to and do my best to live by all the teachings of the Catholic Church as taught by the Pope and the bishops in union with him?*

This third question is the flip side of the previous one. It's important to examine yourself to see not only whether you reject a doctrine or practice of the Faith, but also whether you're making an effort to embrace what the Church teaches.

Note, too, that it isn't necessary for you to comprehend fully each doctrine the Church teaches. As Frank Sheed once put it, "Christ did not become man so that man could become a theologian." Christ simply wants you to do your best to understand the Church's teachings and assent to them freely. For example, not even the holiest Pope or the wisest Father of the Church fully comprehended the doctrine of the Trinity, yet each of them upheld that doctrine and freely assented to it. The same is true of the Church's teaching about the Real Presence of Christ in the Eucharist. No human being has the natural capacity to grasp the vastness of this truth, but we believe it nonetheless because Christ and the Apostles taught it.[67] To reject that teaching of the Magisterium is to reject Christ.[68]

If you don't know your Faith, you risk sharing a defective "Catholicism" that includes things the Church doesn't teach or require. For example, if you haven't educated yourself in the Faith, you may have a sincere, but misguided, conviction that to be truly Catholic, everyone must follow the forms of prayer or piety that you follow or must practice a particular

[67] Cf. John 6:22-71; Matt. 26:26-28; 1 Cor. 11:23-32. For a comprehensive discussion of this doctrine, see James T. O'Connor, *The Hidden Manna*.

[68] Cf. Luke 10:16.

Marian devotion that you practice. With this conviction, you can knowingly or unknowingly communicate a message to non-Catholics that these practices are required of all Catholics.

For example, some women prefer to wear a hair veil or mantilla, a head covering, as a sign of respect when they attend Mass, following the rule in the Western Catholic Church during the centuries leading up to Vatican Council II. In the 1960s, the Church relaxed this rule, so women are no longer required to keep their heads covered during Mass.

Wearing a mantilla is still laudable, of course, and no woman should be discouraged from showing reverence to the Lord in this way. But some women who wear mantillas look down on those who don't. They see this practice as a dividing line between "real" Catholics and those who have "compromised" on the issue of head coverings. I've overheard women comment derisively on other women who don't wear the traditional head covering. In addition to being a sure sign that the sin of pride is flourishing inside, this bad attitude is also a subtle but dangerous stumble down that slippery slope of being more Catholic than the Pope.

There's similar contention over the way Catholics receive Communion at Mass. Some Catholics who receive

Communion in the hand show condescension or even scorn toward those who prefer to receive Holy Communion on the tongue. They look down on Catholics who prefer such traditional piety.

Such attitudes are wrongheaded and deeply uncharitable. Why? Because giving people the impression that being Catholic involves some element that isn't essential — or the opposite error, leading someone astray with the notion that certain essential elements of the Catholic Faith aren't — can warp their understanding of the Church.

Even if you're sincere in your efforts to share the Faith, you can still fall into the trap of being more or less Catholic than the Pope. You may have heard the quip about the person who sincerely believes there's no poison in his cup of Kool-Aid: he may be sincere, but if there *is* poison in his cup, he's sincerely wrong. In spite of his sincerity, he'll wind up sincerely sick, if not worse.

How do you avoid this trap?

Study the Faith. You'll soon learn what the Church does teach and what she doesn't. "If you are to serve God with your mind," said Blessed Josemaría Escrivá, "to study is a grave obligation for you."[69]

---

[69] Blessed Josemaría Escrivá, *The Way* (New Rochelle, New York: Scepter Press, 1985), no. 337.

Search and Rescue

There's no such thing as an "add water and stir" approach to apologetics. You're going to have to prepare yourself the old-fashioned way: you'll have to learn the material.

Here are a number of ways you can prepare yourself for explaining and defending the Faith, so that, when an opportunity presents itself, you'll be ready, willing, and able to engage in your search-and-rescue mission.

~

Get to know Scripture

St. Paul told Timothy, "All Scripture is inspired by God and profitable for teaching, for reproof, for correction, and for training in righteousness, that the man of God may be complete, equipped for every good work."[70] One of the greatest of the "good works" that the written Word of God will equip you for is the search-and-rescue mission that the Holy Spirit has prepared for you personally from all eternity.

The fact is that many Protestants will simply stop their ears and not listen to the case for the Catholic Church if it isn't made from Scripture. So, if you want to be successful in sharing the Faith with your Protestant friends, you'll need to develop some basic Bible skills.

[70] 2 Tim. 3:16-17.

Fortunately, to use Scripture effectively, you don't need an advanced degree in Scripture or a photographic memory. Ninety-nine percent of all the Protestants you meet don't have either. What they do have is an abiding love for the Bible, a love that translates into a familiarity that they can use to their advantage — and, if you don't have a similar love for the Bible and familiarity with it, they can use your ignorance to your disadvantage.

Here are some things you can do to come to know Scripture better:

• *Pay attention at Mass.* Every Mass on Sunday contains four Bible readings, and every daily Mass contains three. Over the course of the Catholic Church's three-year liturgical cycle, you'll hear nearly the entire Bible as it's read from the pulpit.

• *Get in the habit of reading the Bible every day.* God is pleased and glorified when you make an effort to spend at least a few minutes a day studying Sacred Scripture.

Read a chapter a day from the Gospels. Then move on to the Acts of the Apostles and the letters of the New Testament. If you use a good Catholic study Bible, such as the Navarre Bible series, you'll also be able to navigate easily through the Old Testament, which will bolster your understanding of the New Testament. As you read the Old Testament along with the New, you'll see how the New Testament fulfills the Old. Following the Scripture readings for each day's Mass will also help you see the relation of the new Testament to the Old.[71]

Within just a few weeks of Bible reading, you'll experience an increase in your knowledge of the Faith and your confidence in speaking about it. Just imagine how confident you'll feel after a year of steady reading and prayerful reflection on the Bible!

You could begin by focusing your Scripture reading on subjects that concern those you've been evangelizing. Your Baptist brother-in-law, for instance, may not believe in Christ's Real Presence in the Eucharist. Before you speak with him about it, study the biblical evidence for this teaching. There are plenty of supporting passages in Scripture that will help you discuss Christ's Real Presence in the Eucharist. They're not hard to find, and there are books available, such as the *Catechism of the Catholic Church,* that will even

[71] You can find all the readings for daily and Sunday Mass in *Magnificat* magazine or in a daily missal.

show you where particular doctrines are found in Scripture.[72]

• *Supplement your study of the Bible with good Catholic commentaries, papal encyclicals, writings of the Church Fathers, and study guides, especially the* Catechism of the Catholic Church.[73] This will ensure that you understand Scripture according to the authentic interpretation that has been faithfully handed on to us by the Church from the time of the Apostles.

• *Buy a study Bible, and mark it up.* No, I'm not suggesting you deface the Bible! Just find a trustworthy Catholic edition of the Bible — such as the New American Bible, the Navarre Bible series, the Revised Standard Version, the classic Douay-Rheims Bible, or another approved Catholic edition — and use a pen and a highlighter to mark key passages and carefully

---

[72] See my book *Where Is That in the Bible?*; Antonio Fuentes, *A Guide to the Bible*; Henri Daniel-Rops, *Daily Life in the Time of Christ.*

[73] A wonderful new tool for Scripture study is *The Ignatius Catholic Study Bible: The Gospel of Matthew*, the first volume in a series that will cover the entire New Testament. Also consider papal documents on Scripture, such as Pius XII's *Divino Afflante Spiritu*, Leo XIII's *Providentissimus Deus*, and Vatican II's *Dei Verbum.*

add your own notes and cross-references (hint: those
with generous margins are better for this purpose,
because they give you more space to write notes and
cross-references).[74]

Besides making your Bible even more user-friendly,
marking it up in this way will help prepare you for discussions about Scripture: you'll have lots of necessary
information at your fingertips.

• *Use your Bible to help you pray:*

    • *Read prayerfully the Psalms and the canticles,*
    and learn from them how to live in accordance
    with God's will.[75]

---

[74] In my book *Where Is That in the Bible?* I provide
you with, essentially, the apologetics notes and cross-
references I've put in my personal Bible over the years.
This little reference work will save you a lot of time,
and get you started sooner. For more information
about this and other tools that will help you study
Scripture, see the reading plan at the end of this
book.

[75] The Song of Moses (Exod. 15:1-18 and Deut. 32:1-43);
the Song of Hannah (1 Sam. 2:1-10); the Song of
Habakkuk (Hab. 3:2-19); the Song of Isaiah (Isa. 26:
1-21); the Song of Jonah (Jon. 2:2-9); the Song of the
Three Children (Supplement to Dan. 3:3-22); the
Benedicite (Supplement to Dan. 3:35-66); the *Magnificat*
(Luke 1:46-55); the *Benedictus* (Luke 1:68-79); the *Nunc*

• *Reflect on the lives of holy men and women in
Scripture* — such as Moses, Susannah, the
Blessed Virgin Mary, St. Joseph, the Apostles,
and especially Christ Himself — and pray for
the grace and courage to follow their example.

• *Meditate on the virtues that Scripture teaches —
especially in the Gospels and in St. Paul's letters —
and ask the Lord to help you develop those virtues.*

Listening to Scripture at Mass, reading and reflecting
on it, and using it to pray will help you become much more
effective in explaining your Catholic beliefs, but a greater
benefit is the grace you'll receive from the Holy Spirit, who
will nourish and strengthen you through Scripture, which
He Himself inspired for your benefit.

Becoming familiar with the Bible will also help you detect false teaching and misquoting of Scripture when you
encounter it. The principle behind this is used in a secular
context by agents in the U.S. Treasury Department and the
F.B.I. These agents are trained to spot counterfeit bills, not
by studying counterfeit bills, but by spending long hours

Dimittis (Luke 2:29-32); plus these other New Testament canticles: Eph. 1:3-10; Phil. 2:6-11; Col. 1:12-20;
1 Tim. 3:16; 1 Pet. 2:21-24; Rev. 11:17-18, 15:3-4.

studying *authentic* currency. They become so familiar with the real thing that any bogus bill immediately stands out. Likewise, if you study Scripture, you'll be less likely to be taken in by error when it comes your way.

Being able to detect error is important because, although Protestants often memorize Scripture, I've noticed that, to make verses easier to remember, they sometimes condense or misquote them. This practice often leads them into doctrinal errors.

For example, on a Protestant call-in radio program, I was once engaged in a lively debate about the Catholic Church with a Protestant minister. The Protestant tried to use 2 Corinthians 5:8 to disprove the Catholic teaching on Purgatory.[76] He claimed that it says, "To be away from the body [i.e., to be dead] is to be at home with the Lord." He understood this to mean that, if you're dead, you can be nowhere but with the Lord, in Heaven. But he misremembered the verse. It actually says, "Yet we are courageous, and we would rather leave the body and go home to the Lord." In other words, the actual text doesn't exclude the possibility of Purgatory. If I hadn't spent time reading the Bible, I wouldn't have recognized the Protestant's error, and who

[76] This doctrine is covered extensively in my book *Any Friend of God's Is a Friend of Mine*.

knows what damage might have been done to the listeners if
I hadn't corrected it?

☙

Study the Catechism of the Catholic Church

In addition to reading Scripture every day, put yourself
on a catechetics "crash course" that includes regular reading
of the *Catechism of the Catholic Church.*[77] You can even key
your reading in the *Catechism* to the particular Bible passage
you read each day by looking up that Bible passage in the
back of the *Catechism* to see which paragraphs correspond
with it.

☙

Read books and listen to tapes on the Faith

Read Catholic books that will increase your knowledge
of the Faith. Reading one book every week, or every two
weeks, or even every month will dramatically raise your confidence in sharing the Faith, make you hunger to learn more,
and deepen and strengthen your love for Christ and His
Church. Read at your own pace, but read! At the end of this

---

[77] This is made much easier by the fact that the *Catechism*
is arranged by subject, uses succinct, numbered paragraphs for easy reference and study, and includes an excellent and extremely useful index of names, subjects,
Scripture verses, and citations drawn from the writings
of the early Church Fathers.

book you'll find an extensive list of recommended books I've used for years as an apologist.

At the end of this book, I'll give you a basic reading plan that will, in a relatively short time, equip you with all the basics you'll need.

Finally, listen to cassette tapes on Catholic themes and apologetics to supplement your reading. You can do this while you drive or when you work around the house.

⌒

Study Church history

"To be deep in history is to cease to be Protestant": this was the conviction of the Venerable John Henry Cardinal Newman, the English scholar and Protestant convert to the Catholic Church.[78] He knew that history is the weak link in most Protestant arguments against the Catholic Church.

Your Protestant roommate, for instance, may cite certain pre-learned Bible verses to try to disprove a Catholic doctrine or practice, such as infant Baptism or the Real Presence of Christ in the Eucharist. You'll be able to respond more effectively to his Bible-only approach with historical evidence than with a different Bible verse (which

---

[78] Venerable John Henry Newman (1801-1890), *On the Development of Christian Doctrine*.

could quickly lead to a pointless game of "biblical badminton"). Protestants, Jehovah's Witnesses, Mormons, and other non-Catholics are quite often very hazy about the history of Christianity before the Reformation. This affords you an opportunity to use objective, verifiable historical evidence to make a case for Christ and for the Catholic Church. For example, you can show them that issues such as infant Baptism, the sacraments, Purgatory, the development of the canon of Scripture,[79] the Eucharist, and other key doctrinal issues were taught or practiced in the early Church.

Using Church history to evangelize is simple. Just say, "Isn't it reasonable to assume that if you and I are in disagreement about what the Bible means, we should consider how the early Christians understood the Bible?" By showing from the writings of the Church Fathers the marvelous continuity between what we as Catholics believe today and what the early Catholic Church believed and taught, you can make great headway.[80]

---

[79] That is, the list of books that belong in the Bible.

[80] I recommend the three-volume set *The Faith of the Early Fathers*, by William Jurgens. On the Eucharist, see James T. O'Connor's *The Hidden Manna*. On the canon issue, see *Not by Scripture Alone*, by Robert Sungenis, Patrick Madrid, et al.

Search and Rescue

≈

Become familiar with Church Tradition

Tradition is different from Church history. Tradition comprises the religious teachings and practices handed down, written or orally, from the beginning of the Church, aside from what has been revealed through Scripture. Even though they reject the notion of Tradition itself, some non-Catholics, such as Protestants and even Mormons and Jehovah's Witnesses, embrace certain elements of Tradition, such as the canon of Scripture, the apostolic authorship of the Gospels (all of which are anonymous, containing no internal reference to the identity of the author), worship on Sunday instead of on Saturday (the Sabbath), and the cessation of general revelation with Christ and the Apostles.[81] These convictions come from Tradition, not from Scripture.

Yet the canon of Scripture is an extremely powerful example of Tradition that Protestants must accept if they're even to have a Bible. There's no "inspired table of contents" in the Bible that tells us which books belong and which don't. That information was revealed gradually by God to the Catholic Church, and that revelation was eventually quantified and formally codified by the Catholic

---

[81] Cf. *Catechism of the Catholic Church*, par. 65-66. Mormons don't believe in the cessation of divine revelation.

Church in the form of the canon, or list, of books God revealed as divinely inspired. This revelation comes down to us through Tradition, completely separate from the Bible. Without Tradition, we simply wouldn't have a Bible at all.[82]

There are many good books on Tradition. Read some of them to become familiar with examples of Tradition and how to discuss them with non-Catholics.[83] You'll soon be able to help non-Catholics consider the Catholic Church from a different vantage point than they're used to.

Improve your critical-thinking skills

Critical-thinking skills will help you to discern logical fallacies and inconsistencies in the arguments leveled against the Catholic Church (or against the existence of God and divinity of Christ).[84]

---

[82] Cf. Robert Sungenis, Patrick Madrid, et al., *Not by Scripture Alone* (Santa Barbara: Queenship, 1997), 22-23, 267-295.

[83] For a good explanation of the relationship between the Bible, Tradition, and the Church's teaching authority, see the Vatican II document *Dei Verbum*, the Church's dogmatic constitution on divine revelation. Also see my book *Where Is That in the Bible?* and Robert Sungenis, Patrick Madrid, et al., *Not by Scripture Alone*.

[84] Patrick J. Hurley's *A Concise Introduction to Logic* will help you develop critical-thinking skills.

Search and Rescue

Here's an example of how being logical will help you. Many Protestants believe in the doctrine of *sola scriptura* (by Scripture alone), often referred to as "Bible only" Christianity. This position says essentially that all matters of doctrinal importance for Christians are found in Scripture; everything necessary is found in the Bible, so anything not found in the Bible is unnecessary. They argue that, for this reason, the Pope, bishops, the Magisterium, and councils are unnecessary, or at least they're not to be regarded as infallibly authoritative. But if you rely on this logic, Scripture itself can't be authoritative, for nowhere does Scripture say, implicitly or explicitly, that Scripture itself is the sole rule of faith for Christians.[85]

If you sharpen your own critical-thinking skills, you'll spot such illogic and will be better prepared to refute arguments that are illogical, such as *sola scriptura.*

Developing your critical-thinking skills will also help you ensure that the arguments you yourself make are sound. As in the earlier example of the poorly prepared Catholic's defense of Mary's Immaculate Conception, illogical arguments can make Catholic doctrines look silly and can harm listeners. So be logical and consistent when you're explaining and sharing the Faith.

[85] Cf. Sungenis, Madrid, et al., *Not by Scripture Alone*, 19-22.

Study non-Catholic arguments

Be familiar with arguments that non-Catholics level against the Church. Karl Keating's *Catholicism and Fundamentalism,* in which he shows many of the standard arguments raised by Protestants, will help you. Also, *Envoy* magazine contains many excellent apologetics articles that offer point-by-point methodologies for understanding, critiquing, and responding to non-Catholic arguments.

A word of caution: when you study non-Catholic arguments, make sure you do so with support so that you won't be led astray by these arguments. Let your prayer group or a good Catholic friend, your pastor, a priest friend, or your spiritual director know what you're doing ahead of time so that they can support you with prayer and check up on your spiritual situation. The Bible warns about this:

> Two are better than one. . . . For if they fall, one will lift up his fellow; but woe to him who is alone when he falls and has not another to lift him up. . . . And though a man might prevail against one who is alone, two will withstand him. A threefold cord is not quickly broken.[86]

[86] Eccles. 4:9-10, 12.

Search and Rescue

The key advice here is: Don't go it alone! Be sure you have plenty of help in the form of prayer support, accountability, and assistance when you begin to study the arguments of non-Catholic groups.

☞

Learn about non-Christian religious issues

Studying Scripture will help you discuss the Faith with non-Catholics who believe in Christ and the Bible. But what about those who don't? You may know atheists, Buddhists, Hindus, New Agers, agnostics, and even people who believe in a generic "God" but who have been so swamped with the errors of pop-philosophy and self-help spirituality books that they have no idea who God really is or even how they can come to know and love Him.

If you want to want to bring a non-Christian loved one into the Church, be at least moderately informed about the kinds of religious issues that concern them, such as the existence of God (in the case of an atheist), the "problem of evil," the Christian claim that Christ is God, and the claims of the Bible and the Catholic Church.[87]

---

[87] An excellent book for dealing with non-believers and atheists is *A Handbook of Christian Apologetics*, by Peter Kreeft and Ronald K. Tacelli, S.J. It offers useful information and techniques on how to diffuse typical arguments raised by non-Christians, especially atheists.

Keep an evangelization stockroom

Start developing a cache of materials — such as tracts, books, and tapes — that you can give to those who are estranged from Christ or His Church. Not only will these materials be handy references for you, but they'll also help your loved ones begin building a storehouse of knowledge of the Faith.

When I was in grammar school back in the '60s, the nuns who taught me told my class about poor kids who lived in countries where the Catholic Faith had not gained much of a foothold. They needed food and medicine, and they needed to be taught about Jesus Christ. At the start of each school year, the nuns passed out cardboard savings banks to each of us and encouraged us to divert some of our candy and trading-card money each month to be saved in our "missionary bank." At the end of the year, the nuns collected our banks and sent the money that we had saved to the office of the Propagation for the Faith, which coordinates and funds much of the Church's missionary activity in developing countries.

Use a similar program for your own search-and-rescue mission. Start your own home "missionary savings fund." Toss your stray coins and bills into a Tupperware container

or a mason jar — you may be surprised to see how quickly
it fills up. Use the collected money to buy books or tapes
that you can give to others to teach them about the Faith.

☞

Start an evangelization club

Start an informal evangelization club. Members can pool
their money to buy a large quantity of Catholic books, tapes,
or evangelization tracts and then, as a team, pass them out
door-to-door in your neighborhood or in some public place,
such as at the beach or in a park. Granted, "taking it to the
streets" may not be for everybody, but I've seen it work well,
and conversions do happen as a result.

I'm very enthusiastic about using books and tapes to
evangelize because I've seen over the years how effective
they are. Plus, if you're shy, handing your cousin a book
and saying, "Here: Chapter 4 has a good explanation of that
question you asked about Mary," is a lot less intimidating
than having to sit down and give that explanation yourself.
You'll want to be able to explain the Faith eventually, of
course, because evangelization is an interpersonal mission,
and you can answer the personal questions of your cousin
better than a book or a tape can. This is a mission that
each of us as Catholics is called to carry out: "Always be
prepared to make a defense to anyone who calls you to

account for the hope that is in you, yet do it with gentleness and reverence."[88]

But if you're not ready to explain the Faith to others,[89] using books and tapes is a good start while you're preparing yourself. As I said, many conversions to the Catholic Church begin with the gift of a good book or tape. Start your own "missionary" evangelization plan, and you'll see for yourself.

⁓

Practice sharing the Faith

This step is, in my experience, the easiest and the most fun. Practice in sharing the Faith will make the information you read in books and listen to on tapes that much more ingrained in your memory. One way to practice is to recall an argument your coworker has brought up to you against the Catholic Church — such as "The Bible doesn't teach the Catholic doctrine of the Eucharist." Begin by asking yourself where you'd look in the Bible for a passage that speaks about this doctrine. (If you have your study Bible marked up, this

---

[88] 1 Pet. 3:15.

[89] Remember, just because you may not be fully prepared now, don't let that become an excuse to postpone getting prepared! Recognize your need for study as an opportunity for grace — a grace for you personally, and for those whose lives only you can touch. Don't sit back and let this opportunity pass you by.

will be a snap for you! Or refer to one of the books I recommended earlier.) Then think of the kinds of responses to that passage you might get. Rehearse how you'd respond in turn. Using this mental exercise — "If he said this, I would say that" — will also ensure that you'll be prepared when your coworker hits you again with that challenge.

~

Be orderly in studying the Faith

The order in which you study the teachings of the Faith will have a dramatic impact on how well you learn them. (The same is true in your explaining the Faith to others.) Just as you wouldn't try to learn calculus before you've learned the times tables, long division, and algebra, so you shouldn't try to conquer the nuances of biblical interpretation before you've developed a basic knowledge of Church teachings and Scripture, especially the Gospels. Similarly, unless you have a solid grounding in the basics of the Faith, you must not try to plow through theological treatises on the metaphysics of Transubstantiation. First you've got to assimilate the Church's basic teachings on Christ's Real Presence in the Eucharist.[90] Those theological treatises are wonderful,

[90] Two key books to help you do this are Frank Sheed's *Theology for Beginners* and James T. O'Connor's *The Hidden Manna*.

of course, but they're of little use to you if you lack grounding in the teachings on the Eucharist found in Scripture and in the *Catechism*. You may never need to delve into those more technical theological works, but I guarantee that you do need to establish a firm foundation in the basics.

A recent time-management seminar taught me to focus first on the basics. On the instructor's table was a large, empty glass beaker. As the attendees watched, the instructor began carefully to fill the container with softball-size rocks. When the rocks had filled the container to the brim, he asked the class, "Is the container full?" About half the students said yes.

"No," the instructor said. "It's not full." Then he reached under the table, brought out a bag of smaller rocks, and proceeded to dump them into the container. The small rocks tumbled down past the bigger rocks, filling up the gaps between them.

"Is the container full now?" the instructor asked. Some of the students said yes.

The instructor smiled. "No, it's not full." Then he poured a bag of small gravel into the beaker, and the gravel fell into the remaining small gaps between the large and small rocks. The instructor's question came again: "Is it full now?"

Scattered laughter broke out among the students. Some said yes, others no. "It's not full yet," the instructor said with a sly grin, and he brought out a bag of sand, which he poured into the container. A collective "ahhh" rose from the class as they watched the fine granules trickle into all the empty spaces in the beaker and rise to its very edge. This time, when the instructor asked, "Is it full now?" they responded with an enthusiastic "Yes! Now it's full."

"No, it's not full yet," the instructor said as he brought out from under the table a large container of water. As he slowly poured the water into the container, the students realized they had been mistaken again. The water gradually filled the container, completely filling every pocket of air. When the water had reached the brim, the instructor leaned over his desk toward the students and said, "Now it's full."

"Now, what does this exercise teach us about time management?" he asked the class, his eyebrows raised in anticipation.

The students said that the beaker represented a day, and filling it with all the different things shows how much activity can really be packed into a day.

"Wrong again." The instructor replied, smiling mischievously. "It shows that if you want to get all those things into the container — big rocks, small rocks, gravel, sand, and water — you have to start with the big rocks. If you try any other sequence, you'll never be able to get it all in."

Likewise, you must start your efforts to deepen your understanding of Catholic teaching with the "big rocks" of the Faith: the Trinity, the Incarnation, God's love for us, salvation, and the reality of Heaven and Hell. Then you can move on to the finer points of Catholic doctrine, such as the Eucharist, the Communion of Saints, Purgatory, Marian doctrines, the sacraments, the relation between Tradition and Scripture, and the papacy.

As you study the Faith (and even as you explain it to others), think like a builder. Start at the foundation, and work your way up, level by level. Doing this ensures a solid, stable structure.

Equip yourself to take advantage
of different opportunities

You know the old saying: "Expect it when you least expect it." This is good advice for the search-and-rescue apostle. You never know when you'll face an opportunity for sharing the Faith. Preparing yourself for your search-and-rescue mission by studying and by gathering materials will equip you to be ready, willing, and able to take advantage of unexpected opportunities to draw souls to the Church.

These opportunities vary. A very brief opportunity to explain and share the Faith calls for a markedly different approach than does an opportunity that affords you several hours, weeks, or even years to do so.

Let's say the woman ahead of you in line at the grocery-store checkout notices your prolife pin or T-shirt and makes a derogatory comment about your trying to "impose your morality" on others. It's quite possible that this woman is suffering from guilt and remorse for an abortion she had. Since you don't have a lot of time, offering her an extensive list of quotes from the Church Fathers on the evils of abortion or providing a volley of Bible verses showing the sanctity of unborn life[91] aren't viable options. The right tool might be a prolife pamphlet or fact-sheet (a few of which you keep stashed in your purse or wallet for exactly this sort of encounter, of course). Combined with a silent prayer for her, a sincere smile, and a few well-chosen, nonconfrontational words about why you believe that killing unborn children is wrong, the simple reading material you offer this woman can be a catalyst for God's grace to begin working in her heart.

On the other hand, you might answer your door on a Saturday afternoon to find a pair of smiling Mormon missionaries on your doorstep. Their goal is to persuade you that the

---

[91] Cf. Isa. 44:2, 24, 49:1-5; Eccles. 11:5; Jer. 1:5, 20:15-18; Hos. 12:2-4; Luke 1:39-44.

Catholic Church offers a "false gospel,"[92] that the Mormon
Church is the true church, and that you should therefore
become Mormon. In this situation, unlike your brief encounter with the woman in the checkout line, you may have an
hour or more to present your case for Christ and the Church.
Here you'll need a basic knowledge of Scripture (Mormons
are interested in discussing the Bible), historical evidence,
and logic: tools that cut through the bogus theological and
scriptural arguments the Mormons will offer you.

One afternoon, I was standing in line at a busy Kinko's
copy center, waiting to pay the cashier for copies I had made
of a flyer announcing a Catholic apologetics seminar. Out of
the corner of my eye, I could see a man standing behind and
to the left of me. He was reading over my shoulder. What he
read prompted him to tap me on the shoulder.

"Excuse me, but I couldn't help but notice the word *Catholic* on those flyers you have there. What are they all about?"

I explained, looking at my watch and feeling antsy because I was already running late and needed to get those
flyers to the FedEx drop box before the last pickup that
afternoon. But this man wanted to talk about Catholicism,

---

[92] Cf. 1 Nephi 13:5-6; also cf. Bruce R. McConkie, *Mormon Doctrine* (Salt Lake City: Deseret Books, 1958 ed.),
314-315.

right then and there. He introduced himself as Andy. It turns out he was a former Catholic turned Evangelical Protestant, and the pastor of a local church, to boot. He wanted to show me from the Bible why I was "in the wrong Church." With a sigh, I went out to my car and got my Bible (it blew him away that a Catholic would have a Bible with him), while Andy held my place in line.

When I got back, I paid for my flyers, and then we stood there in the middle of that busy copy center, Bibles in hand, engaged in a friendly but very animated discussion about the Catholic Church. You can imagine the stares we got from those who came and went around us. ("A couple of religious weirdos," some probably thought to themselves.)

This chance conversation resulted in a long-term chance for me to explain and share the Catholic Faith with Andy. Over several years, through our discussions, he abandoned much of his earlier anti-Catholicism and even began to con-sider coming home again. And although he hasn't converted (yet) to the Catholic Church, he did tell me that our "acci-dental" meeting at the copy center was a turning point in his life, the very first time he had encountered a Catholic who was willing and able to discuss the Bible with him.

In summary, study your Faith, try to have apologetics materials (and your Bible) on hand, and learn to expect the unexpected. Then, when search-and-rescue opportunities arise, you'll be ready to answer Christ's call to draw souls to Him.

⌒

Begin today

Start preparing for your search-and-rescue mission today. As I said, your initial steps are simple. First, pick up your Bible and begin reading it. Second, spend a few minutes each day studying the *Catechism*. Third, regularly read good Catholic books and listen to tapes that explain Church teachings that your loved ones have questions about. Even if you can find only a few minutes to do it here and there, the more you study the Faith, the more you'll know about it. The more you know about the Faith, the more effectively you'll be able to explain it and win for Christ those who are separated from Him and His Church.

Ask yourself now

• How well do I know my Faith? Which areas do I need to study further?

• Can I distinguish between the beliefs and practices that all Catholics must adhere to and those that are optional?

Search and Rescue

• If I were to face an opportunity to share the Faith today, would I be ready?

Search-and-rescue action agenda

• Set aside some time each day to read Scripture.

• Set aside some time each day to read the *Catechism*.

• Ask the Holy Spirit to help you understand elements of the Faith that you don't understand.

• End your resolutions with the following prayer:

> Ineffable Creator, who,
> from the treasures of Your wisdom,
> have established three hierarchies of angels,
> have arrayed them in marvelous order
> above the fiery heavens,
> and have marshaled the regions of the
> universe with such artful skill,
> You are proclaimed the true font of
> light and wisdom, and the primal origin
> raised high beyond all things.
> Pour forth a ray of Your brightness
> into the darkened places of my mind;
> disperse from my soul the twofold darkness

into which I was born: sin and ignorance.

You make eloquent the tongues of infants.

Refine my speech, and pour forth upon

my lips the goodness of Your blessing.

Grant to me keenness of mind,

capacity to remember,

skill in learning, subtlety to interpret,

and eloquence in speech.

May You guide the beginning of my work,

direct its progress, and bring it to completion.

You, who are true God and true man,

who live and reign, world without end. Amen.[93]

---

[93] Robert Anderson and Johann Moser, trans. and ed., *The Aquinas Prayer Book* (Manchester, New Hampshire: Sophia Institute Press, 2000), 41, 43.

Chapter 6

Learn how to approach others

"If you truly want to help the soul of your neighbor,
you should approach God first of all with your heart.
Ask Him simply to fill you with charity,
the greatest of all virtues; with it
you can accomplish what you desire."

St. Vincent Ferrer

You now understand that, to be successful in your search-and-rescue mission, you have to curb your ego and develop the heart of an apostle. You've listened, you've prayed, and you've studied. Now you have to begin talking. I know from experience that it can be hard to figure out just where to begin and then how to proceed, so I'd like to share with you some techniques and approaches that have worked well for me and for others.

Let me begin by telling you about what may initially seem to be a hopeless search-and-rescue case. Once you see how easy it is to find ways to begin and to proceed, I think you'll be encouraged.

Find common ground

While flying from Chicago to San Diego a few years ago, I was seated next to a very pleasant gentleman from India. As a practicing Hindu, he was eager to tell me about the merits of his religion, and I was happy to learn more about it (so I could be more effective when talking to Hindus about Christ). For over three hours, we discussed his religion. I listened attentively to his explanations, learning about his beliefs and gaining time to formulate a response and decide which tools would work best for me to share my Faith with him. Once he had given a thorough presentation of the case for Hinduism, I began to explain my Catholic beliefs.[94]

I began by pointing out the areas of his religion that I could agree with. There weren't many, but I was able to find at least a bit of common ground. The fact that he, a Hindu, and I, a Catholic, could at least agree on basic things such as the importance of prayer and trying to live a moral life was a starting point.

When you talk with non-Catholics, even non-Christians, always search for common ground first, however modest it might be. Common ground is the foundation on which you can build your bridge to their hearts and minds. By showing at the outset that you're willing to acknowledge that elements of goodness and truth exist in their religion, you create an environment in which dialogue becomes easier.

[94] It's important not to interrupt when a non-Catholic is making the case for his beliefs. Patient, attentive listening shows respect and will greatly improve your chances of getting a fair hearing, free of interruptions, when it's your turn to explain what you believe.

St. Paul was a master of this approach. While visiting
Athens, the center of Greek paganism, he strolled through
the Areopagus and saw numerous shrines and temples to
various Greek and foreign gods.

> Paul, standing in the middle of the Areopagus, said,
> "Men of Athens, I perceive that in every way you are
> very religious. For as I passed along, and observed the
> objects of your worship, I found also an altar with this
> inscription: 'To an unknown god.' What therefore you
> worship as unknown, this I proclaim to you."[95]

Notice that Paul didn't blast the idol-worshiping Greeks
with a theological howitzer, ripping into them for not wor-
shiping the one true God. Instead, he began his search-and-
rescue mission by finding common ground with the pagans.
He offered honest praise: "I perceive that in every way you
are very religious." He showed a desire to understand their
beliefs: "For as I passed along, [I] observed the objects of your
worship." Finally, he affirmed something valid and tried
gently to correct their error of polytheism: "I found also an
altar with this inscription: 'To an unknown god.' What
therefore you worship as unknown, this I proclaim to you."

[95] Acts 17:22-23.

Search and Rescue

In just a few words, Paul disarmed his pagan audience and opened a door through which he could bring them the Good News of Jesus Christ. And it worked. "Some mocked; but others said, 'We will hear you again about this.' [And] some men joined him and believed."[96] St. Paul's technique will work for you, too. Look for common ground, and build on it.

Let's go back to my in-flight conversation with the Hindu. Quoting Bible verses to him would have had about the same effect as quoting from the Yellow Pages, because, as a Hindu, he didn't regard the Bible as authoritative. So I spoke to him first about my belief that Jesus Christ wasn't merely a wise teacher or a holy prophet, but that He is God. I shared with him some of the objective, verifiable historical evidence that, about two thousand years ago, a man named Jesus was born and lived in Palestine, that He claimed publicly to be God, that He claimed publicly that He would establish a Church that would last until the end of the world, that He claimed publicly that He would rise from the dead, and that His followers, who claimed to be eyewitnesses to that Resurrection, also testified publicly (and usually under pain of persecution, torture, and sometimes even execution) that He rose from

[96] Acts 17:32-34.

the dead.[97] These were historical facts this man hadn't heard or considered.[98]

Most important, I explained, Christ, who is God, also promised that salvation comes through Him alone. I gently but firmly invited the Hindu man to pray to Jesus Christ and ask Him to speak to his heart about the truth of His divinity and His unique mission as Savior.[99] The Hindu had never been presented either with these facts or with this message from a Catholic, and I sensed from his reactions and his thoughtful expression that he would ponder the claims of

[97] A brilliant and easy-to-follow presentation of this objective evidence and the logical conclusions that follow from it is found in Peter Kreeft and Ronald K. Tacelli, S.J., *A Handbook of Christian Apologetics* (Downers Grove, Illinois: InterVarsity Press, 1994), 150-221.

[98] Scripture can be useful for demonstrating how many Old Testament prophecies about the Messiah were fulfilled in Jesus Christ, but even the antiquity of those prophecies will have little power to impress a Hindu or another non-Christian if you haven't first laid the groundwork with a different tool: the historical evidence that a man named Jesus did in fact exist. For a basic overview of these prophecies, see Cornelius Hagerty, C.S.C., *The Authenticity of the Sacred Scriptures* (Houston: Lumen Christi Press, 1969), 85-107.

[99] "I am the way, and the truth, and the life; no one comes to the Father, but by me" (John 14:6); "There is salvation in no one else, for there is no other name under Heaven given among men by which we must be saved" (Acts 4:12).

Search and Rescue

Christ long after we parted company in the airport terminal. We shook hands and exchanged business cards as the plane was landing. A few days later, I followed up by sending him a copy of Frank Sheed's marvelous apologetics book *Theology and Sanity* with a note thanking him for our conversation.

I never heard back from him, but that's okay. Knowing that God's grace works in mysterious ways, I won't be at all surprised to bump into him in Heaven (if, by God's grace, I find myself there), where he will tell me how his conversion to Christ and the Catholic Church all started with a chance conversation on a night flight between Chicago and San Diego.

By starting with the objective historical evidence, I laid a solid foundation for the case for Christ and increased the likelihood that my non-Christian acquaintance might consider with an open mind the biblical evidence I presented later. Although this search-and-rescue opportunity might have seemed impossible initially, by first listening to the Hindu man and then by simply finding some common ground with him, I was more easily able to begin speaking about Jesus Christ and the Catholic Church.

There are other ways to find common ground, especially when you're dealing with Mormons, Jehovah's Witnesses, and Evangelical Protestants, many of whom are former

Catholics. If you suspect that this is the case, you'll be surprised at how many doors that will open for you.

I was once in an apologetics discussion with a Protestant minister on an nationally aired, Evangelical call-in radio program. I sensed that one of the Protestants who called in might be a former Catholic, so I asked him, "Were you once Catholic?"[100] It turns out he was. "Alex" had left the Church as a young adult and had been firmly entrenched in his Protestant rejection of Catholicism for ten years. In spite of the pugnacious way he questioned me on the radio show, I was able to understand where he was coming from better than I would have if I hadn't known that he used to be Catholic. That allowed me to tailor my approach and to zero in on some of the issues I knew would resonate with him.

By God's grace, this approach worked.

That afternoon, after the show, Alex called me at my office, and we spoke for over an hour about his objections to the Catholic Church. Since I knew he was a former Catholic, I started and ended our discussion by inviting him to

---

[100] I recommend this form of the question as opposed to the more pointed "Are you an ex-Catholic?" because addressing someone as an "ex-Catholic" can have a derogatory or condescending connotation.

"come home." He needed and wanted solid answers to his objections, but he also needed to hear, as all former Catholics do, a sincere invitation to return to the Church. We stayed in contact through letters and phone calls, and I sent him a package of Catholic apologetics books and tapes to help him grapple with his questions. Within six months (thanks to God's grace and mercy), he had returned to the Church, made a good confession, and had his marriage blessed and his young children baptized. He told me later that it was my question "Were you once Catholic?" that had struck a chord in him during the radio show and opened the door for him to consider returning to the Church.

Use this technique, and you'll be surprised at how often you'll meet people who have left the Church. Knowing their background will help you help them come home.

☙

Redirect the conversation

A few years ago, some Jehovah's Witnesses came to my home to share their message that Armageddon was right around the corner and that the only way to avoid being annihilated was to leave the Catholic Church and become a Jehovah's Witness. I knew from experience that they were well-trained, as all active Jehovah's Witnesses are, to deluge me with a complicated patter of Bible verses and historical details that Jehovah's Witnesses believe support their theories. The prefabricated, lock-step approach to their door-to-door efforts affords them a measure of confidence that a Catholic answering the door doesn't usually have.

Knowing this, I used a technique that's especially helpful in discussions with door-to-door missionaries who have canned presentations. I call it "redirection": I politely steer the conversation away from their prepared presentation and into a theme of my choice.

This approach is particularly helpful when you're explaining and defending your Faith to someone who wants to convert you to his religion or philosophical system — folks such as Mormons, Jehovah's Witnesses, aggressive Evangelical Protestants, and others who roam residential neighborhoods, usually in groups, seeking to convert anyone who'll open their front door and listen to their message. Here's how redirection works.

It's Saturday afternoon, and you're busy doing something very important, such as watching *Gilligan's Island* reruns or taking a nap. The doorbell rings. You open the door to see a pair of smiling gentlemen from the local Calvary Chapel (a large Evangelical Protestant "Bible church"). They shake your hand warmly, introduce themselves as Chuck and Jeff, and slip you a glossy, four-color brochure promoting their church's programs and worship services. As they launch into their presentation, just redirect the conversation:

Chuck: "Thanks for taking a few minutes to chat with us."

Jeff: "That's right, we're in the neighborhood today talking to folks about Jesus Christ. We'd like to share with you from the Bible how you can be saved and how, when you die, you can go to Heaven to be with Jesus for all eternity!" (He opens his well-worn Bible and points to a passage.) "Look what it says here in John 3 . . ."

You: "Hey, this is fantastic! I'm so glad you guys are here! I've been wanting to ask someone from your church a question." (Your exuberance catches them off guard, and Jeff pauses in mid-sentence, not sure what to make of your broad smile.) "Is your church, Calvary Chapel, the church that Jesus Christ established two thousand years ago?"

Jeff: "Um, uh . . . what do you mean?"

You: "What I mean is, it says here in Matthew 16:18 . . . " — you flip Jeff's Bible open to that chapter — "that Jesus founded a specific Church, one that He said He would build on a 'rock.' Is Calvary Chapel that church?"

You have redirected the conversation into an area that *you* want to discuss: the Church. Regardless of what they say in response, you've moved them away from their rehearsed presentation, and now you can begin directing them to Bible passages you want to share with them — verses that speak about the Church Christ established and how to determine which church that is.[101] In this way, using redirection, you take control of the discussion and require them to confront evidence they may not have seen before.

☞

The Socratic Method

Another very useful technique is the Socratic Method. It's not only easy to use, but fun, and usually yields good results. The idea behind the Socratic Method is to ask a series of questions that will lead the other person to the conclusion you want him to see. These questions will elicit a truth from the very person who denies that truth.

For instance, if your neighbor tells you, "I believe that the Bible is the sole, sufficient, and infallible rule of faith for Christians," ask in response, "Why do you believe that?" He might answer, "Because the Bible says so." Respond with

---

[101] For a detailed list of Bible verses to use in discussions on this and other topics pertaining to the Catholic Church, see my book *Where Is That in the Bible?*

another question: "Where does the Bible say that?" When he looks for it, he'll discover that the Bible doesn't say that anywhere.[102] In this way, without having to explain or defend the issue yourself, you've politely but firmly led him to the truth of the matter by helping him to see the illogic of his position.

Let's say you're at the annual family-reunion picnic, and you're standing at the barbecue chatting with your brother-in-law Larry who left the Catholic Church a few years ago and is now an ardent Evangelical Protestant.

"Why did you leave the Catholic Church?" you ask.

Larry: "Because it doesn't teach the Bible, and I want to be in a Bible-teaching church."

You: "How do you know the Catholic Church doesn't teach from the Bible?"

Larry: "Because when I was a Catholic, I never heard anything about God's Word — just a lot of stuff about man-made traditions."

You: "What about those lengthy sections of the Old and New Testaments that are read and preached on at Mass? Isn't that teaching from the Bible?"

Larry: "Well, it's not the same."

---

[102]For an introductory discussion of this topic, see Sungenis, Madrid, et al., *Not by Scripture Alone*, 1-29.

You: "Why not?"

Larry: "At my church, the preacher teaches what's in the Bible — nothing more, nothing less."

You: "How do you know that your preacher's interpretation of the Bible is correct?"

Larry: "What do you mean?"

You: "I mean, how do you know he's right in the way he interprets a given verse? Say, the verse where Jesus says, 'I am the bread of life. . . . My flesh is food indeed, my blood is drink indeed.'[103] Or where He takes bread and wine and says at the Last Supper, 'This is my body, this is my blood.'[104] How does your preacher interpret those verses?"

Larry: "Jesus was speaking figuratively there, not literally, as you Catholics believe."

You: "How do you know He wasn't speaking literally?"

Larry: "It's clear from the text."

You: "But other Protestants, such as Anglicans and even some Lutherans, think that He was speaking literally. What about their interpretations? How do you

[103]John 6:35, 55.
[104]Cf. Matt. 26:26-28; Luke 22:19-20.

know they're not right and your preacher isn't wrong?"

Larry: "Well, I just know he's right. The Anglicans, the Lutherans, and you Catholics are wrong."

You: "Is your preacher infallible?"

Larry: "No, but he doesn't need to be; the meaning of Scripture is plain."

You: "But if its meaning is plain, why do many Anglicans, Lutherans, and Catholics misunderstand its meaning so badly?"

Larry: "Well . . . "

You can see how this technique works. You simply keep asking questions, leading the person to see the flaw or problem with his position. The value of this approach is that you aren't put on the defensive, you don't have to scramble to defend your Catholic beliefs (although there's definitely a time and place to defend them), and the person you're evangelizing is forced, perhaps for the first time, to re-examine his beliefs and attitudes.

Use common sense

Often the most powerful way to help someone see the truth is basic common sense. Overcoming someone's objections to a teaching of the Catholic Church can be as simple as pointing out an obvious fact they haven't noticed. That's often easy to do when you combine Scripture with common sense.

Take, for example, the commonly heard argument that Catholics worship statues. Your non-Catholic coworker Jill reads you Exodus 20:4-5, where God tells Moses not to carve any graven image as an idol and not to worship it. To Jill, the Catholic Church appears to be violating that command by its use of statues, crucifixes, and other "graven images." Use logic to show that this understanding is wrong. Point out that in other Bible passages God actually explicitly approves of or even commands the carving of religious statues.[105] Soon Jill will see that God doesn't condemn statues per se: He condemns idolatry.

As another example of what I mean, use common sense in the "call no man father" argument. Jesus said, "Call no man your father on earth, for you have one Father, who is in Heaven."[106] To Protestants, the Catholic practice of calling priests "father" seems to be a clear example of disobeying

---

[105]Cf. Exod. 25:18-20, 26:1; Num. 21:8-9; 1 Kings 6:23-28, 7:23-29. For a basic explanation and defense of this Catholic teaching (and other aspects of the Communion of Saints), see my book *Any Friend of God's Is a Friend of Mine* (San Diego: Basilica Press, 1996), 95-100.

[106]Matt. 23:9.

what Jesus says in the Gospel. By citing the many Bible verses in which St. Paul, St. Stephen, and St. John refer to others (or themselves) as "father," you can demonstrate that Christ didn't mean that we shouldn't use the title "father" for priests and others in authority and that the Bible doesn't forbid this practice.[107]

Learn to spot such logical fallacies in people's arguments. Once you do, you'll have great success in clarifying the fuzzy thinking that often hinders others from coming closer to Christ and His Church.[108]

Appeal to human experience

Sometimes the only way to reach someone with the Truth is first to appeal to his own experience. Everyone knows how it feels to despair, to be lonely, to be hungry, to be lost or frightened. Christ often spoke about these human sufferings and linked them to His message. He encouraged the fearful with His promise of protection and guidance. To

---

[107] Acts 7:1-2, 38-39, 44-45, 51-58; Acts 21:40, 22:1; Rom. 4:16-17; 1 Cor. 4:15; Philem. 1:10; 1 John 2:13-14.

[108] I recommend the following books to help you become adept at using logic and common sense in your "search-and-rescue" mission: Montague Brown, *The One-Minute Philosopher*; Patrick J. Hurley, *A Concise Introduction to Logic*; and Peter Kreeft and Ronald K. Tacelli, S.J., *Handbook of Christian Apologetics*.

those who were grieving, He promised joy and healing; the Beatitudes[109] are a powerful example of this.

In the same way, following the Lord's example, you can help your family and friends come closer to Christ and the Church by recognizing their sufferings and telling them how prayer, the sacraments (especially Confession), and Christ Himself will ease their sufferings and sustain them in their trials. Jesus promised: "Come to me, all who . . . are heavy laden, and I will give you rest."[110]

As I mentioned earlier, many women (both non-Catholics and former Catholics) are suffering from the guilt and anguish caused by abortions and sterilizations. For them, the doctrinal or biblical arguments they raise in opposition to the Catholic Church may be a shield to protect them from confronting and dealing with the pain of abortion. I've been in many situations where a woman's problem with the Church springs from an abortion she has had. In these instances, I've learned to offer a very gentle response, speaking about Christ's loving forgiveness, how He wants us to come home and be forgiven and reconciled with Him. In these situations (like many others similar to this), you should speak gently but

[109]Matt. 5:3-12.
[110]Matt. 11:28.

with conviction about the great gift of the sacrament of Reconciliation and how God wants to heal us of our past sins. "All this is from God, who through Christ reconciled us to Himself and gave us the ministry of reconciliation.... So we are ambassadors for Christ, God making His appeal through us. We beseech you on behalf of Christ, be reconciled to God."[111]

Also, offer your family and friends examples of those souls, such as St. Augustine, who have overcome adversity through God's grace. Many people won't be persuaded by Bible verses or quotations from the Church Fathers, but they'll be touched and convinced when you show them that in Christ and His healing mercy, all the answers to their most serious problems can be found, and their wounds healed.

~

Strive for reconciliation

Some people struggle not so much with the ravages of unrepented personal sin, but with the scandal inflicted on them by Catholics. Earlier I told you about Eric, who was scandalized and led into homosexual behavior by an actively homosexual priest. You can use Christ's parable of the weeds and the wheat to show people like Eric, who have come to

[111]2 Cor. 5:18, 20.

think all Catholics are immoral and hypocritical, why God sometimes permits scandal in His Church.

> Another parable He put before them, saying, "The kingdom of Heaven may be compared to a man who sowed good seed in his field; but while men were sleeping, his enemy came and sowed weeds among the wheat, and went away. So when the plants came up and bore grain, then the weeds appeared also. And the servants of the householder came and said to him, 'Sir, did you not sow good seed in your field? How then has it weeds?' . . . The servants said to him, 'Then do you want us to go and gather them?' But he said, 'No; lest in gathering the weeds you root up the wheat along with them. Let both grow together until the harvest; and at harvest time I will tell the reapers, 'Gather the weeds first and bind them in bundles to be burned, but gather the wheat into my barn.' "[112]

Use this parable to remind those like Eric that God doesn't typically "uproot" scandalous Catholics, but lets them continue in their ways. Nonetheless, even though these bad Catholics can cause damage, God is still in charge

[112]Matt. 13:24-30.

and will not let them ultimately defeat those members of the Church who are striving to live holy lives.[113]

Think about this for a moment. Perhaps you yourself may have, knowingly or unknowingly, scandalized a friend or relative who now thinks to himself, "She calls herself a Catholic, but look how she lives; look how she treats people!" If so, perhaps you have some repair work to do with that person. Ask God for the graces to rebuild bridges where they have been demolished through your own bad example or that of others.

It also may be that you're not at fault for something your family member or friend holds against you; in that case you can still seek to make peace and achieve reconciliation through a humble effort to forgive and be forgiven. "Put on then, as God's chosen ones, holy and beloved, heartfelt compassion, kindness, humility, gentleness, and patience, bearing with one another and forgiving one another, if one has a grievance against another; as the Lord has forgiven you, so must you also do."[114]

⌒

Let God do the talking

Several years ago, I was conducting an apologetics conference at a parish in Michigan. During the afternoon

---

[113]Cf. Matt. 18:6.
[114]Col. 3:12-13; cf. Matt. 6:14-15, 18:21-22.

question-and-answer session, an elderly man in the audience approached the audience microphone and related how he had been away from the Catholic Church for thirty-five years. The several hundred people in the audience listened attentively as he described his journey into anti-Catholicism, a journey that began with a falling out with his parish priest. Whatever it was that caused the dispute, the man stormed out of the Church and lived for all those years with a deep sense of rage and bitterness against the Catholic Church and Catholics. He took every opportunity to harangue Catholics and criticize the Church. For thirty-five angry years, he stayed away from the sacraments and lived a life of hardened sin.

One day he met a young Catholic whom, like many who had come before, he subjected to a withering anti-Catholic rant. This young fellow simply listened, nodding now and then, saying nothing. When the older man had run out of steam, he expected the Catholic fellow to launch back at him with a defense of the Church.

But the young man didn't.

He didn't argue or change the subject to something less confrontational. He simply put his hand on the former Catholic's shoulder, looked him in the eye, and said gently, "Well, I'm not sure what to say to you in response to all that. You obviously were very hurt by what happened many years ago.

But I can tell you this: you're always welcome to come home to the Catholic Church. It doesn't matter how long you've been gone or what you've done in the meantime; you can come home, if you want to. The door is always open to you."

As the elderly man got to that point in his story, he became choked up with emotion. Others in the audience were moved by his simple, humble testimony. Through his tears, he finished his story by saying that the encounter with that young Catholic man was a miracle of God's grace in his life. It was as if a ray of warmth had suddenly begun to melt the ice that had encased his heart for so long. His anger and rage against the Catholic Church began to evaporate, and he felt a deep longing to come home.

And that's what he did. That very day, this elderly man made his way to a local parish and went to Confession for the first time in over thirty-five years. He began attending daily Mass and rebuilding his lost Faith. He didn't say what became of the young Catholic man who helped him come home, but he told us that it was his marvelous and mysterious response that began the healing work of grace in his soul. This was a beautiful example of what Proverbs tells us: "A gentle response turns away wrath."[115]

[115]Prov. 15:1.

Learn how to approach others

He finished his story with the remark that, had it not
been for that young man's simple, mild response in the face
of animosity, he might still be living in his prison of anger,
estranged from the Church and away from the sacraments.
That was for me a profound insight. Clearly, that young man
had received a special grace from God to say the right thing
at the right time. It was certainly an extraordinary moment
of grace.

If you look for them, you'll find that opportunities for
grace are all around you. God wants to give you the necessary gifts and graces to help you reach out in this way to your
loved ones with the Truth. Always be warm and welcoming;
sometimes, as in the case of the young man I just told you
about, the words you speak won't be coming from you, but
from the Lord, who, if you let Him, will speak through you.
I'm positive that the young man who gave such a mild and
penetrating answer had no idea he was being used by God
in that instant as such a powerful instrument of healing and
reconciliation.

The same is true for you. You may never realize how pow-
erfully God will use your words and actions for the benefit of
those around you. The key is to remember that the Lord has
designs for helping those in your life, and He wants to use
you as an important part of His mysterious plan.

Search and Rescue

⌒

Simply radiate Christ's love

Let's go back to your Uncle Joe, who's living with his girl-friend and who cares only for worldly things. You won't reach him with biblical arguments. You've got to offer him authentic Christian friendship; you have to take a "hate the sin but love the sinner" approach to his lifestyle. When opportunities arise, try to draw him back to the things of the Faith. Invite him to join you at Mass or to come to a family Baptism. He's an ex-Catholic, so he might be moved by serious questions such as "What is the meaning of life?" "Where are you going?" "What can you expect after you die?" You might even try to raise the topic of Hell in nonconfrontational ways, to make him think about the eventual eternal consequences of his actions.

Don't be afraid to be direct, too. If an opportunity arises to talk to your Uncle Joe about Jesus Christ and His love for him, be bold. Watch and pray for an opportunity.

Christ said, "As the branch cannot bear fruit by itself, unless it abides in the vine, neither can you, unless you abide in me. I am the vine, you are the branches. He who abides in me, and I in him, he it is that bears much fruit, for apart from me you can do nothing."[116]

[116]John 15:4-5.

By all means, don't flaunt your Christianity or your prayer life as if it were a fur coat or a flashy ring. That's a major turn-off. Instead, let the warmth and light of your love for Christ (and His love for you) radiate quietly from you when you are in Joe's presence. Show from your own life as well as from the things you say and do that the true happiness Joe yearns for is found only in Jesus Christ. You'll be amazed at how even the smallest, seemingly imperceptible things can be used by God to draw dissolute former Catholics back home. I've seen it happen.

When opportunities present themselves, talk about how God intends for each of us to be free and happy, how our sinful choices in life inevitably lead us into a self-induced slavery to sin, and how Christ came to save us from our slavery, to liberate us with the truth.[117]

If you sense that your Uncle Joe is beginning to feel the weight of guilt and remorse for his sinful choices, you might ask him to read the parable of the Prodigal Son.[118] Many Catholics who return to fervent spiritual life and regular practice of their Faith have told me that reading this passage at a crucial moment, when God's grace was beckoning

---

[117]"The truth will make you free" (John 8:32).
[118]Luke 15:11-32.

them, shattered their complacency and brought them to their senses.

⌒

Try different approaches

You see, you have many effective tools and techniques to use in your search-and-rescue mission. Don't worry if you haven't developed skill in using one or another of them. While you're developing one skill, use the others. Hand your brother a book or a tape that explains an objection he has to the Faith. Show your friend how the Church will solve her problems and meet her needs. Use as many tools and techniques as you can. The more you use them, the better you'll be able to use them, and the more successful your search-and-rescue missions will be.

Ask yourself now

• Which technique would be most effective in drawing my loved ones to the Faith?

• Am I warm and sincerely welcoming toward non-Catholics? Or am I oblivious and apathetic toward them?

• Do I ask God to tell me how to respond to search-and-rescue opportunities and then listen for His answer? Do I prayerfully invite the Holy Spirit to guide my words and even speak through me?

Search-and-rescue action agenda

◆ Determine which techniques will be most effective for sharing the Faith with your loved ones.

◆ Ask God to help you see opportunities to use those techniques.

◆ Meditate on these words of St. Paul on finding common ground with others: "I have made myself a slave to all, that I might win the more. To the Jews I became as a Jew, in order to win Jews; to those under the law I became as one under the law — though not being myself under the law — that I might win those under the law. To those outside the law I became as one outside the law — not being without law toward God but under the law of Christ — that I might win those outside the law. To the weak I became weak, that I might win the weak. I have become all things to all men, that I might by all means save some. I do it all for the sake of the Gospel, that I may share in its blessings."[119]

[119] 1 Cor. 9:19-23.

Search and Rescue

• End your meditations and resolutions with the following prayer:

> Lord, grant that I may always
> allow myself to be guided by You,
> always follow Your plans,
> and perfectly accomplish Your holy will.
> Grant that in all things, great and small,
> today and all the days of my life,
> I may do whatever You require of me.
> Help me to respond to the slightest
> prompting of Your grace, so that I may be
> Your trustworthy instrument, for your honor.
> May Your will be done in time and eternity —
> by me, in me, and through me. Amen.[120]

---

[120]"Prayer of St. Teresa of Avila": *Manual of Prayers*, 220.

Chapter 7

Now it's time to begin

"Whoever has been called
to the preaching of the gospel
should obey instantly
and without delay."

St. Basil the Great

When I was in eighth grade, a large swimming-pool complex opened near our home in Southern California. Part of a huge sports and recreation center that was open to the public, the pool complex became an immediate magnet for kids from all over, including me. It was in that pool, on my very first visit, that I learned a very important lesson about apologetics and evangelization — although, at the time, I had no idea I was learning anything.

It was hot and sunny that afternoon as my mom pulled the station wagon up to the curb and a bunch of us bathing-suit clad kids piled out, deliriously excited by the knowledge that we'd spend the next few hours cavorting (without parental supervision; that was the best part) in those clear blue waters that beckoned us from beyond the fence.

This pool was absolutely huge. Rightly classified as an "Olympic" swimming pool, it was equipped with several diving boards at one end, the highest of which stood more than thirty-two feet above the surface of the water.

Search and Rescue

From my vantage point in the water, that diving board looked like fun — nice and high, but not too high for me to try. "It's gonna be awesome to do a cannonball from that height," I thought to myself as I clambered out of the water and made my way to the ladder. Besides, other kids — mostly kids older than I — were lining up to jump off, so I knew it had to be fun.

I climbed the ladder, and, when the kid in front of me had disappeared off the end of the long, blue board, it was my turn. I walked slowly to the edge of the diving board and got ready to jump.

That's when it hit me just how high this high-dive really was. From the water, it had looked impressively high. But now, as I stood there, way, way above the pool, a wave of fear swept over me. I felt as if I were standing a hundred feet over the water. I felt as if I were about to jump out of an airplane. I was scared.

The boy behind me on the ladder obviously had read my fear. He called out, "Hey, kid. What are you scared of? Go ahead and jump."

I turned back toward the ladder to climb down. "I changed my mind," I stammered sheepishly.

"No!" he said, grinning. "Don't be afraid. It's fun. Go ahead."

I stood there, frozen in fearful indecision. I glanced around and realized that a lot of kids, in and out of the pool, were now watching me standing there like an idiot.

"Jump," he said again, goading me. "Come on. Just do it, man. It's not gonna hurt you."

Still I hesitated.

"Just do it!" he called out.

I turned around, closed my eyes, held my breath, and jumped.

It was like jumping out of an airplane — scary but exhilarating. When I came up for air, I knew I had to do it again. I was hooked.

Yes, it was frightening, jumping off that high dive, but it was also fun. And I had learned to conquer my fear of jumping. That felt good, too.

I spent the next hour leaping from that diving board, over and over, my heart pounding and my stomach flying into my throat — and loving it. But I never would have experienced that exhilaration if I hadn't taken that very first step.

⌒

Don't let fear stop you

One of the biggest mistakes Catholics make when it comes to sharing the Faith is that they don't share the Faith.

Search and Rescue

That's probably a mistake you're making, too. You think
about it; you imagine how good it would be if you did it.
You hear the still, small voice of grace telling you to speak
up and be an apostle to your family and friends. You may
even surround yourself with apologetics books and tapes. (Is
this book another one of them?) You're thrilled with the *idea*
of talking to others about Christ and the Church. But that's
as far as you go. You stand at the edge of that high-dive, but
you don't jump.

If this sounds like you, you know what you have to do.

You have to just do it. Take the plunge, if you'll pardon
the pun.

That kid's advice — "just do it" — is the core principle
you need to embrace if you're going to share the Faith effectively with your non-Catholic loved ones.

I don't mean that you've got to start talking this minute,
before you've prepared yourself spiritually and intellectually;
as I said earlier, that could lead to harm. I mean that you've
got to stop thinking that evangelization is somebody else's
job and start making it your own.

You've got to make a serious effort right now to quit
yielding to those excuses that keep you from this work to
which God is calling you. Consider the wise counsel of Fr.
Marcial Maciel, L.C., the founder of the Legionaries of

Christ: "We do not have the right to shield our light, the light of Christ, when so many people live in darkness. We have no right to haggle over our love and self-giving when the eternal salvation of souls it at stake. We have no right to withdraw into our passivity when the urgency of the good and the Church's needs are so compelling."

⌒

We all make excuses

It's a fact: the single biggest impediment to sharing the Faith is the excuse we conjure up just at the moment we're supposed to begin. Admit it.

And the excuses are as old as the hills. God has heard them all before, and if He didn't accept them from others, why do you think He'll accept them from you?

Let's look at a few of the excuses you've probably used:

• *Excuse one: "Lord, you've got the wrong person."*
A few times, you've probably shirked your obligation to try to draw your loved ones into the Church by claiming that you're unqualified. After all, evangelization is a job for priests, nuns, catechists, and guys like Patrick Madrid, right?

Wrong.

Moses tried this excuse when God asked him to lead His people out of slavery in Egypt to freedom in the Promised

Search and Rescue

Land: "Who am I that I should be the one to go to Pharaoh and lead the Israelites out of Egypt?"[121]

And God answered, "I will be with you."

Today God is asking you to rescue a soul who has left the Catholic Church or has never known the freedom of the Catholic Church — and He promises to be with you. Don't forget this when you worry about the risks involved in talking to others about Christ. Sure, you may be worried that you'll get clobbered in the discussion and humiliated in the process. You may fear that you're too shy, you lack eloquence, and you don't have ready answers to people's objections to the Faith. But if you think you're the wrong person for a search-and-rescue mission, you've forgotten what God said to Moses in the same circumstances: "Don't worry. I will be with you."

Because if God has chosen you for this search-and-rescue mission, you're the right person; and if God is with you, what further qualifications do you need? "Cast yourself into the arms of God," says St. Philip Neri, "and be very sure that if He wants anything of you, He will fit you for the work and give you strength."[122]

[121]Cf. Exod. 3:11.

[122]Thigpen, *A Dictionary of Quotes from the Saints*, 109.

• *Excuse two: "What authority do I have to do this?"*

You're likely to make this excuse when you're faced with an opportunity to talk about the Faith with someone who knows you well, someone who knows your faults and weaknesses. You worry that he will say, "Who are *you* to tell me about all this? You're not perfect, yet you think *you're* qualified to tell *me* about God? Get real."

Moses tried this excuse, too: "If I come to the people of Israel and say to them, 'The God of your fathers has sent me to you,' and they ask me, 'What is His name?' what shall I say to them?"[123] Moses feared that the Israelites would reject him because they would think he was acting on his own authority. What authority did Moses himself have, after all?

Notice God's response to this excuse: "Say this to the people of Israel: 'I AM has sent me to you. . . . The Lord, the God of your fathers . . . has sent me to you.' "[124]

When those close to you ask of you — as Christ's own neighbors and friends asked of Him[125] — "Who do you think you are?" remember that, unworthy though you are, you are still God's messenger. He chose you for this mission. When you speak to your cousin Mark, who has left the Catholic

[123] Exod. 3:13.
[124] Exod. 3:14-15.
[125] Cf. Matt. 13:54-57.

Church to become a Fundamentalist, or to your friend Pam, who has simply stopped going to Mass, let each of them know that you're not offering them a new message. Rather, you're reminding them of something they were taught in their youth — something they know, deep down in their hearts, to be true (even if they won't admit it to you).[126] If your loved ones have drifted away from God because of a divorce and invalid remarriage, because of an abortion not repented of, because of some other sinful life-style choice, or simply through apathy, reminding them of what they know to be true and inviting them to embrace it once again can have great spiritual impact.

So when your loved ones accuse you of being a "holier than thou" know-it-all and when they ask what authority you have to speak to them about God, tell them that you're simply reminding them of something they already know. This response does two things:

- It saves you from having to prove that you're not being "holier than thou."

- It leaves the door open for you to emphasize (lovingly and with patience, of course) what they know

[126]1 Cor. 4:5; Heb. 4:13.

in their hearts: they've departed from the truth they
once held.

> • *Excuse three: "What if they*
> *simply ignore what I'm saying?"*

This excuse is understandable, but irrelevant. It really
means that you don't trust that God will act in a way that
will help the person you're evangelizing to see the truth of
your message. Remember: you're only planting the seed —
in what might seem to you like infertile, inhospitable soil.
But don't worry. It is God who will give it growth.[127] Your
friend may ignore or even reject your words today, but God
can later lead him to reflect on them more deeply and see
the truth in what you said.

Believe it or not, Moses tried this one, too: "But behold,
they will not believe me or listen to my voice, for they will
say, 'The Lord did not appear to you.' "[128]

The Lord's response? He told Moses that He would work
miracles through him as a means of convincing Pharaoh,[129]
who was holding God's people in slavery. Pharaoh certainly
did not accept Moses' message when he delivered it to him.

[127]Cf. 1 Cor. 3:7.
[128]Exod. 4:1.
[129]Exod. 4:2-9.

Search and Rescue

He spurned Moses and then ignored him. But God stepped in, as He promised, and sent plagues that made Pharaoh change his mind. God made the Egyptian king an offer he couldn't refuse: "Let my people go, *or else.*"

Now, in the ordinary course of events, this isn't the means God uses to accomplish His will, but it isn't unheard of for miraculous events to happen in the lives of ordinary people. Ask God to give you the grace to do whatever He wants done in your search-and-rescue mission. It may be that God will work a miracle that will manifest His power — although it may be a hidden one, known only to the soul you've been sent to rescue.

Keep in mind that, in most instances, God doesn't use miracles to get people's attention and stimulate their faith in Him. Remember what Christ said to Doubting Thomas the apostle: "Have you believed because you have seen me? Blessed are those who have not seen and yet believe."[130] Sometimes God simply offers someone His grace and waits for a response. So pray for the person you are sharing the Faith with. Ask God to bestow His grace on him in a way that will open his eyes as well as his heart.

[130]John 20:29; cf. John 4:48.

• *Excuse four: "I don't have the training*
to speak to people about You, God."

This is an easy way to avoid sharing the Faith with others. Many times I've heard people say, "I'd like to be able to talk about Christ and the Church with others, but I get nervous and tongue-tied." How many opportunities for grace pass you by because of this excuse!

Guess who else made this excuse. Yes, Moses again: "Lord, I have never been eloquent, neither in the past . . . nor now that You have spoken to Your servant; but I am slow of speech and tongue."[131]

Of all Moses' excuses, this is the lamest. I think God agrees: you can almost hear the exasperation in His voice when He responds, "Who gives one man speech and makes another deaf and dumb? Or who gives sight to one and makes the other blind? Is it not I, the Lord? Go then! It is I who will assist you in speaking and will teach you what you are to say."[132]

What God says to Moses He says to you, too.

Consider Mother Teresa of Calcutta. She has been widely recognized as a saint and she converted many, yet she wasn't

---

[131]Exod. 4:10 (New American Bible version).
[132]Exod. 4:11-12 (New American Bible version).

what people typically think of as eloquent. She drew others to Christ with her simple, humble, direct way of teaching and defending the Faith, without using fancy words or sophisticated rhetoric.

God used Mother Teresa, and He wants to use you, too. Whether or not you're eloquent may be an issue for you, but it isn't for God. Remember what He told Moses: "It is I who will assist you in speaking and will teach you what you are to say."

• *Excuse five: "I'll do it next time."*

How many times I have used this excuse myself! This is the Big Enchilada of excuses, the one you're apt to fall back on when no other cop-out comes to mind. It allows you to salvage a little bit of self-esteem and still avoid having to evangelize. "I'm going to do it, at some point," you reassure yourself, "just not right now. I'll do it next time." The problem with saying, "I'll do it next time" is that you have no way of knowing whether there will be a next time, either for the person you're trying to reach or for you. Opportunities pass, never to present themselves again; people die suddenly or are lost to you for other reasons. So don't put it off; you may never have a chance to help this person again.[133]

[133]Cf. Job 8:9, 9:25-26; 14:5; Ps. 103:15-16.

Think often about this caution from St. James: "Come now, you who say, 'Today or tomorrow we will go into such and such a town and spend a year there and trade and get gain'; whereas you do not know about tomorrow. What is your life? For you are a mist that appears for a little time and then vanishes. Instead you ought to say, 'If the Lord wills, we shall live and we shall do this or that.' "[134]

And there's another problem with this excuse. Saying, "I'll do it next time" is really just a slightly more dignified way of saying, "I don't feel like doing it right now."

In my work as an apologist, I have to travel by plane frequently. This is where I often find myself falling into the excuse I'm most prone to: "I don't feel like doing it right now." It's one of the temptations I struggle with, because in airplanes I have a chance to get into a conversation with the person sitting next to me, and I know that sooner or later it will get around to the subject of Christ and the Catholic Church.

Sometimes I sit in my seat ready and willing to engage in conversation; sometimes I don't. If you travel by plane much, you know that when you get settled in your seat, if the person next to you is at all talkative, he or she will almost always ask you two questions: What's your name, and

[134]James 4:13-15; cf. Ps. 103:15-16.

what do you do? The first question is easy for me. But the second question is harder. If I'm willing to get into a conversation, when the person asks, "What do you do?" I say, "I'm a writer." Of course, the next question is "What do you write?" And we're quickly into a conversation that can be steered toward the Faith.

But if I'm feeling lazy and don't want to be bothered with a conversation, or if I have a good book that I'd rather read, then, when the person asks, "What do you do?" I reach slowly into my briefcase, pull out my Bible, and lean toward him with an intense gaze. "I'm glad you asked." I say with a smile, "I'm a Catholic *evangelist*." (I've heard others recount similar experiences.) Then, of course, I can read that book, because the person has very quickly decided he's not all that interested in knowing what I do.

Now, this isn't always bad; each of us needs some leisure. But do you know what? When I do that, I miss forever the chance to speak to that person about Christ. I won't ever have a next time.

• *Excuse six: "I don't want to."*

This excuse may lie behind all the others, or perhaps it's a combination of all the others: "I'm lazy and afraid and unsure of myself. I'm not the right person for this job. And when you get right down to it, God, I really don't want to go on this mission for You."

Moses tried to get away with this: "If you please, Lord, send somebody else!"

The Lord's reaction was predictable: He became angry with Moses.[135] Yet, in spite of all Moses' objections, God was willing to reassure him one more time. He promised that He would provide Moses' brother, Aaron, to be Moses' speaker, his mouthpiece. Aaron was an eloquent speaker.

Today, in your own life, God has given you many "Aarons" that you can use to share and defend the Faith: numerous books, tapes, and videos that you can confidently hand to a friend or coworker. If you're not yet comfortable speaking to others about Christ, pray that you'll develop the courage and willingness to do so, and, while God is cultivating that courage in your heart, let books and tapes do the speaking for you.

Each year, as I travel the country giving lectures and apologetics seminars at parishes and universities, I meet people who tell me how they abandoned their former anti-Catholicism and became Catholic all because someone had started the divine chain-reaction of grace by handing them a good Catholic book or tape.

[135]Exod. 4:14.

Search and Rescue

When God provided Moses with Aaron's assistance, He not only reinforced His commitment to help Moses in this difficult mission; He also emphasized how important it was to Him that Moses in particular be the one to carry out this mission. This is as true for you as it was for Moses.

Just think of it!

From all eternity, God, the Lord of the universe, has been thinking about you specifically, knowing that you will play a unique and vital role in His drama of salvation. He has chosen you specifically to bring His message of truth and life to those around you. Regardless of your state in life, God has a plan for you to be a search-and-rescue apostle in His name. But He won't force you: you must choose it yourself. And then you must just do it.

⌒

Ask, seek, and knock

There are lots of other excuses you can make: I'm too old; I'm too young; I'm too shy; I don't have time; I'm not prepared; I'm too busy; I don't want to look like a religious fanatic; religion is a private affair between God and me; it's not right for me to force my religion down someone else's throat.

Face it: they're all just excuses. God is calling you to a search-and-rescue mission, and whatever your hesitations, you've got to stop making excuses and just do it.

Just doing it will help you conquer your fear of being
rejected or ridiculed — even though, chances are that you
won't be rejected or ridiculed at all. Usually, you'll find that
people are pleasantly surprised and open to hearing about
your Catholic beliefs and your love for Christ.

There's nothing wrong, of course, with telling God your
fears and hesitations — after all, He knows them already,
and He wants to shower you with good things, the things
that will draw you closer to His heart.

One of those good things He wants to give you is a
spirit of humble courage and a willingness to be a visible
"city on a hill," a light to those around you.[136] He said,
"What father among you, if his son asks for a fish, will instead of a fish give him a serpent; or if he asks for an egg,
will give him a scorpion? If you then, who are evil, know
how to give good gifts to your children, how much more
will the heavenly Father give the Holy Spirit to those who
ask Him!"[137]

If you ask Him, He'll give you the grace of courage in
the face of what seems difficult or impossible. He'll help you
to become like St. Peter, who stepped out of the boat and

---

[136]Cf. Matt. 5:14-16.
[137]Luke 11:11-13; cf. Matt. 6:25-34.

walked toward Christ on the surface of the lake: "[Jesus] spoke to them, saying, 'Take heart, it is I; have no fear.' And Peter answered Him, 'Lord, if it is You, bid me come to You on the water.' He said, 'Come.' So Peter got out of the boat and walked on the water and came to Jesus."[138]

Nevertheless, we all fear to make that first move — as I did, standing high up on that diving board, with nothing but air between me and the water, way down there. "There are a great number of Christians who would be apostles . . . if they were not afraid," said Blessed Josemaría Escrivá. "They are the same people who then complain, because the Lord — they say! — has abandoned them. How do they treat God?"[139]

But don't be afraid . . . and don't be afraid to fail. All success comes from God. As the Lord said, "Apart from me, you can do nothing."[140] But as He did with Moses, He has promised to provide you with the graces you need to be a true apostle, regardless of your state in life, so that, with the help of the Holy Spirit, you can reach those who have wandered away from the Catholic Faith and you can lead them

---

[138]Matt. 14:27-29.

[139]Blessed Josemaría Escrivá, *Furrow* (London: Scepter Press, 1987), no. 103.

[140]John 15:5.

home again. Say now with confidence and joyful humility, "I can do all things in Him who strengthens me."[141]

Ask God for the graces you'll need to speak effectively to your non-Catholic loved one or coworker. If you ask God for His help, He'll give it to you. He promised, "Ask, and it will be given to you; seek, and you will find; knock, and the door will be opened to you."[142]

Ask Christ for the graces you need to reach that person you know who is far from Christ, away from the sacraments, or estranged from the Church — He will give them to you. *Seek* out that person who's wandering far from the Lord — you will find him. *Knock* gently at the door of that person's heart — it will be opened to you so that God's grace can pour in and transform him.

Then take a deep breath now, and just do it. Start sharing the Faith. It's much easier than you think.

When you stand tall and stop hiding behind your excuses for not sharing the Faith, you enter into the mystery of God's Providence. That's when you can begin to accomplish great

---

[141] Phil. 4:13.

[142] Matt. 7:7; read also 7:8-11: this passage reminds us of how God wants to give us all good things, and He wants us to come to Him, as children to their loving father, to ask for them. God delights when we intercede for others, petitioning Him on their behalf (cf. 1 Tim. 2:1-3).

things for Christ, because you're willing to speak to others about Him. Then you can finally make real all those unique moments of grace and conversion in which God has, from all eternity, chosen you to be an instrumental part.

If you say no, the opportunity will pass, perhaps forever.

If you say yes . . . well, just look at what happened when Moses finally said yes to God's plan. Against all odds, in spite of all his excuses, in the face of Pharaoh's armies and power, Moses rescued the people of Israel from their bondage of slavery in Egypt — all because, in the end, he abandoned his excuses and said, "Here I am. Send me!"

Ask yourself now

+ Am I making excuses so I can avoid the search-and-rescue mission that God is asking me to undertake? Am I hesitating out of fear or laziness?

+ Do I trust that God will help me in my search-and-rescue mission if I accept it?

Search-and-rescue action agenda

+ Tell God about your fears in undertaking your search-and-rescue mission, and ask Him to grant you peace and confidence.

• Begin by praying for your friend or family member today, by name.

• Reflect on these words of Christ: "Do not be anxious how or what you are to answer or what you are to say; for the Holy Spirit will teach you in that very hour what you ought to say."[143]

• Reflect on these words of Moses: "Be strong and of good courage . . . for it is the Lord your God who goes with you; He will not fail you or forsake you."[144]

• End your meditations and resolutions with the following prayer:

God, our Father,
we are exceedingly frail and indisposed to
every virtuous and gallant undertaking.
Strengthen our weakness, we beseech You,
that we may do valiantly in this spiritual [task];
help us against our own negligence and cowardice,
and defend us from the treachery of our unfaithful hearts,
for Jesus Christ's sake.[145]

[143]Luke 12:11-12.
[144]Deut. 31:6.
[145]"Prayer of St. Thomas à Kempis": *Manual of Prayers*, 244.

Chapter 8

Don't grow discouraged

"Entrust yourself entirely to God.
He is a Father, and a most loving Father at that,
who would rather let Heaven and earth collapse
than abandon anyone who trusted in Him."

St. Paul of the Cross

"Patience is the companion of wisdom": when he said this, St. Augustine knew what he was talking about. For years this great bishop engaged in a difficult search-and-rescue mission to the fallen-away Catholics in his diocese who had gotten caught up in heresy. He knew that to rescue them, he had to remain calm in the face of their emotional arguments and belligerent anti-Catholicism. His patience and tranquility served as eloquent testimony of his confidence in what he said. It helped convince them that he was speaking the truth and enabled him to lead them home to the Church.

You yourself know from experience how important patience is, how much you appreciate it when others are patient with you, and how hard it can be to stay calm when dealing with difficult situations or people, especially the people with whom you live or work.[146]

[146]I had to laugh when I wrote this line. As I was typing it, two of my younger children came knocking at the door of my home office, asking me for some silly thing they

Search and Rescue

When it comes to search-and-rescue missions, patience
is essential. With it, you can more easily win your family to
Christ and the Church; without it, you're likely to drive
them further away.

Imitate St. Augustine: the more obstinate and irritating
your non-Catholic friends become in their jibes against the
Church, the more patient you must become. I know this isn't
easy, so in this chapter, I'll share with you some techniques I
used to help me stay patient with family and friends I'm trying to bring home to the Church.

The first thing to keep in mind is that, as Mother Teresa
said, "It's between you and God":

People are often unreasonable, illogical, and self-
centered. Forgive them anyway.

If you are kind, people may accuse you of selfish,
ulterior motives. Be kind anyway.

If you are successful, you will win some false friends
and some true enemies. Succeed anyway.

> could have gotten for themselves in the kitchen. I
> shouted back in exasperation, "Get it yourselves, and
> leave me alone! I'm working!" I lost my patience with
> two little people I dearly love just as I was in the very
> act of giving you advice about being patient. What a
> sense of humor God has in showing us our need to curb
> our impatience!

If you are honest and frank, people may cheat you.
Be honest and frank anyway.
What you spend years building, someone may destroy
overnight. Build anyway.
If you find serenity and happiness, others may be
jealous. Be happy anyway.
The good you do today, people will often forget
tomorrow. Do good anyway.
Give the world the best you have, and it may never be
enough. Give the world the best you have anyway.
Why?
Because, in the final analysis, all of this is between
you and God. It was never between you and them
anyway.

⌒

Learn from the saints how to be patient in adversity
The saints are wonderful examples of patience in the
face of opposition, persecution, and rejection. You can imitate them in your own day-to-day encounters with family
and friends. Read their biographies, especially those of St.
Augustine and St. Francis de Sales.[147] Read also the Acts of

[147]See, for example, *The Confessions of St. Augustine* and Michael de la Bedoyere, *Saintmaker: The Remarkable Life of
St. Francis de Sales*.

the Apostles and the letters of St. Paul, which reveal Paul's patience in the trials he faced as an apostle of Christ.

Consider the martyr St. Stephen, the first Christian to die for the Faith.[148] *Martyr* means in Greek "witness" or "one who gives testimony." St. Stephen was a martyr for the truth. Even though his listeners rejected his testimony and were even willing to kill him because of it, he continued to speak out fearlessly.

What can you learn from St. Stephen?

First, remember that, whenever you make an effort to share the Faith with your family and friends, especially in situations where you suffer ridicule, scorn, or rejection as a result, you're a "martyr" for Christ. You simply have to expect rejection. Remember Christ's words: "If they persecuted me, they will persecute you."[149] If your family and friends reject you, take courage in knowing that you're following in Christ's footsteps.

Second, when you're tempted to lose your patience with those who like to snipe at the Pope and the Church, think about St. Stephen's prayers for his killers as he was being stoned: "Lord, do not hold this sin against them!"[150] If God

[148]Cf. Acts 7.
[149]John 15:20.
[150]Acts 7:60.

was willing to grant St. Stephen the grace to be patient while others were *killing* him, He's certainly willing to grant you — if you ask Him — the grace to be patient when others are merely annoying you.

I realize that it's easy for me to tell you to "just be patient," especially when you know that I don't have to endure your Protestant brother, whose arguments against the Catholic Church make your blood boil. But I'm not being glib or doling out advice that I don't take myself. I have family and friends who have left the Church or who refuse to consider the case for the Church. I know very well how tempting it is to make a snide comment when a relative annoys me with his rhetoric or refuses to listen (and I'm sorry to admit I've given in to that temptation more than a few times).

Since we all face the same struggle to keep our emotions in check, take comfort, as I do, in the fact that even great saints like Augustine, Paul, and Francis de Sales had to work to be patient and, because they relied on God to help them, were able to do so. I guarantee that if you remember St. Augustine's remark — "Patience is the companion of wisdom" — and follow his example, you'll be much more effective in explaining, defending, and sharing the Catholic Faith.

Search and Rescue

⤳

Learn techniques for being patient

In addition to recalling the examples of the saints and using the classic technique of counting to ten before you speak, try these simple, effective ways to help you curb your anger and become more patient with others when you talk to them about the Faith:

• *Pray silently for the person during your discussion with him.* Whether he's receptive, or apathetic, or even belligerent toward you, pray for him. Ask God to bless him with the graces he needs to understand and accept the truth. You'll be amazed at how calming this will be for you.

• In addition to extemporaneous prayers that well up in your heart, use these quick prayers that I've found helpful:

Jesus, I love You. Save this soul.

Jesus Christ, Son of God, Savior,
help me win this soul for You.

Holy Mary, Mother of God, pray for this sinner
now and at the hour of his death.

- *Imagine that Christ is right beside the person*, smiling at him with gentle love. Try to look at him through the eyes of Christ and with His love. Ask Christ to flood you with His own patient love for this soul.[151] Remind yourself that Christ loves him as much as He loves you — so much that He died on the Cross for him. Remind yourself that if Christ was willing to die for him, surely you should be willing to be patient with him.[152]

- *Remember the parable of the unforgiving servant*.[153] Christ said that if we want God to be patient with us, we must be patient with others. Remember especially this phrase: "I forgave you all that debt because you besought me; and should not you have had mercy on your fellow servant, as I had mercy on you?"[154] God has been very patient with you, a sinner. Ask Him to give you the grace to be patient with this soul whom He has called you to help.

- *Smile when the person speaks to you;* don't frown or scowl. Nod your head attentively, and show that

[151]Cf. 2 Cor. 5:20.
[152]Cf. 2 Pet. 3:9.
[153]Matt. 18:21-35.
[154]Matt. 18:32-33.

you're sincerely trying to listen and understand his position, even if you don't agree with it. Often, when people see that you're listening to them, they'll calm down. So will you.[155]

☞

Patience may be particularly
necessary with family members

Chances are, the most challenging, unreceptive people you'll encounter in your search-and-rescue efforts will be your own family members. It's common for Catholics to be able to draw their friends and coworkers, and even total strangers, into the Catholic Church, yet be completely ignored by family members. I know this from experience, and I'm sure you do, too.

Let's face it. None of us enjoys being presented with information that requires us to admit we're wrong about something. Much less do we enjoy it when that information is delivered by a close relative. So it shouldn't surprise you that the people closest to you will most likely be the least receptive to your efforts to share the truth with them.

Jesus Himself ran into this problem when he preached the Good News to His own kin and townsfolk in Nazareth:

[155]Cf. Eph. 4:1-2.

And when Jesus had finished these parables, He
went away from there, and coming to His own country He taught them in their synagogue, so that they
were astonished, and said, "Where did this man get
this wisdom and these mighty works? Is not this the
carpenter's son? Is not His mother called Mary? . . .
Where then did this man get all this?" And they took
offense at Him. But Jesus said to them, "A prophet is
not without honor except in his own country and in
his own house." And He did not do many mighty works
there, because of their unbelief.[156]

◠

Don't be discouraged when they don't listen to you
If Christ Himself was rejected by His own kin, don't be
surprised if you get the cold shoulder or vacant stare from
your son or daughter or cousin with whom you're trying to
share the Faith. I know a good Catholic man with several
grown children, who loves his family very much. He has told
me more than once that his children simply won't listen to
him on matters pertaining to the Church. They'll listen to
others who have no credibility, but they give their own dad
the cold shoulder when he tries to talk to them about the

---

[156]Matt. 13:53-58; cf. Mark 6:4.

Search and Rescue

Faith. This man understands that this is a cross he must bear and that, in offering it up, the graces he wins for his children will help them, even if it means they'll continue to ignore his efforts, yet are receptive at some point to the efforts of a total stranger.

In your own case, your Protestant sister-in-law Jennifer may be the sweetest, most loving person you know, except when the subject of religion comes up at family gatherings. It's not that she ceases to be sweet and loving, but you can see that slight, tight-lipped frown as you invite her to come to the apologetics conference your parish is sponsoring.

You've seen that look before, such as when you handed her a book of conversion stories by former Protestants who became Catholic. Using your most disarming smile and low-key manner, you told her that you hoped she'd read the book so that you and she could talk about the issues raised by these converts. Glancing at the cover, she thanked you unenthusiastically with the same tight-lipped frown.

Months went by. When you got up the nerve to ask her what she thought of the book, she brushed off your question by saying she couldn't find the time to read it.

No thanks, no explanation, nothing. Jennifer simply wasn't going to look at information you gave her about the Church, mainly because *you* gave it to her.

Sound familiar?

I'm sure that you've been through similar frustrating experiences with people you love. You want to share with them the truth about Christ and His Church, yet they seem disinterested at best and sometimes even irritated that you would try to "convert" them. Don't let it get you down, and don't give up. Remember that you may be planting seeds that will bear fruit later. In the meantime, ask God to open their hearts to His grace.

⌒

Why they won't listen to you

If you understand why your own family resists your search-and-rescue efforts, you'll be less likely to become discouraged and you'll be able to remain patient and to use a more effective approach with them. Here are some of the reasons they may not listen to you.

• *They may misconstrue your motives.* Your family might see in you a real or imagined "holier than thou" attitude. Why? Because your message that they belong in the Catholic Church implies, at least in their eyes, a tacit "I'm right and you're wrong" kind of superiority. You may not feel that way, but they could well think you do. So be careful not to feed this misconception by being haughty or argumentative with your relatives. In their eyes, the only thing worse than a prophet from within their own midst is a pushy, supercilious prophet from within their own midst.

You may be humble and sincere, but your cousin may see you as arrogant because you want to "convert" him. You give your grown daughter a Catholic videotape to encourage her return to the sacraments, and she thinks you're treating her like a kid. You politely challenge your Fundamentalist uncle to explain why he believes Christians should go by the Bible alone, and he gets offended because you're trying to "force your religion" on him.

When you approach your family members, be prepared for them to attribute to you motives that you don't have. Ask God to give you the grace to be genuine and charitable in your dealings with them. I promise you: you'll be far more successful in winning them to the Faith if you come across as authentic and friendly.

• *They can't be objective toward you.* Your family members know you (or they think they know you): your faults, your mistakes, and your shortcomings. Your parents and older relatives have known you since you were in diapers, so you're in the same situation as Christ was at Nazareth. Rather than give you a fair hearing, your non-Catholic family members may know you too well to hear your message objectively.

• *They may be nursing old wounds or resentments.* These old wounds — which have nothing to do with God or religion — can easily distort your family's judgment of you and of what you say, and they can complicate any effort to talk to them. If your nephew still quietly resents you for the time, years ago, when you shouted at him for denting your car with his bike, that resentment may make him unreceptive to your efforts to get him to go back to Church. You may have no idea that he harbors this attitude toward you, and his lack of receptivity can seem puzzling and strange.

Don't underestimate the power of such hidden dynamics, positive and negative, that may be at work in your family. With this awareness, you'll be much more serene and unflappable when your family members are cold or irrational toward you. Don't forget what Jesus said about His own kinfolk: "A prophet is not without honor, except in his own country, and among his own kin, and in his own house."[157] Imitate His example: do your best to share the Faith with your family, and if they resist you, don't grow angry or let it get you down. Love them with the love of Christ, and be patient. God will act.

*Don't presume that you'll be able
to reach your family members*

It may be that you're not the person who, in God's Providence, will be able to reach your non-Catholic family members. Just as Christ Himself was hindered in His mission to His own family and friends by their obstinacy toward His message — " 'Where then did this man get all this?' And they took offense at Him" — your family may not readily accept your message. This doesn't mean, of course, that you shouldn't try to reach your family members. Even if God doesn't use you to convert them, He may desire to use you to plant spiritual seeds that will bear fruit when someone else reaches out to share the Faith with them.

So pray for your non-Catholic family members. Ask God to send them an effective messenger to lead them home. That messenger may be you, but chances are, some "unknown apostle" outside your family will be better able to do this job.

[157]Mark 6:4.

The Lord knows which is best. Trust in His wisdom, and you will be at peace over this.

It happens all the time in the Bible. God once sent the apostle Philip into the desert to meet an Ethiopian eunuch who was a court official of the Queen of Ethiopia. The eunuch was puzzling over a passage of Scripture, and God sent Philip to him to explain that it referred to Christ. The eunuch was converted and baptized on the spot. Then, just as quickly as He sent Philip there, God sent him away to preach the Good News elsewhere.[158] You can't foresee what messenger, like Philip, God may send to your family members.

So begin praying today, right now, that God will send a "Philip" into the life of your family member who is estranged from the Catholic Church or who has never been Catholic and looks on the Church with suspicion or contempt. I guarantee that if you ask with faith and persistence, God will send the right person into your relative's life to lead him home to the Church. Whether that person is you or someone else isn't important. Your task is to do what you can to rescue him, and if the only thing you can do is pray, that's fine — so long as you do it, starting right now.

[158] Acts 8:26-39.

Search and Rescue

⁀

Leave things in God's hands

Elisabeth Leseur,[159] a holy Parisian woman whose cause for canonization has been entered in Rome, had to rely almost completely on prayer in her search-and-rescue mission — and it was extremely effective.

Elisabeth married Felix Leseur, a wealthy medical doctor and Parisian dandy who, after their marriage, determined to destroy Elisabeth's faith by forcing her to read the skeptical and atheistic authors who had formed him intellectually. Although Elisabeth was by temperament drawn to a life of prayer and austerity, her husband forced her to go with him to parties and gala balls wearing diamonds and furs and to enter into atheistic conversations that she found offensive.

Elisabeth resolved to match the energy of his efforts to destroy her faith with an increase in her own prayers for him and her devotion to him. In all things that were not sinful, she yielded to Felix, all the while living a simple life of love and interior spiritual austerity, without ever letting him know that she was doing so.

Near the age of forty, Elisabeth was diagnosed with a fatal disease, and after some months, she died. After her death,

---

[159] 1866-1914.

Felix, who had had his eyes opened to her goodness by the way that she bore her final sufferings, discovered Elisabeth's secret spiritual diary in which she had detailed the crosses that her husband had laid on her and how she had responded to them with love and sacrifice.[160] Overwhelmed by this revelation of Elisabeth's holiness, Felix returned to the practice of his Faith and, just a year or so later, entered the seminary and was soon ordained a Dominican priest.

In her lifetime, Elisabeth never saw the results of her search-and-rescue efforts. But she persevered in them nonetheless, trusting that the results would come in God's time.

St. Paul, too, often encountered rejection from his own brothers and countrymen, the Jews, when he told them about Christ. Let our Lord's words to Paul encourage you: "Do not be afraid, but speak and do not be silent; for I am with you."[161]

The same goes for you! Don't be afraid to talk to your family members about the Faith. Be patient and calm and, above all, unwavering in your loving commitment to complete your search-and-rescue mission, even if it takes a lifetime of quiet, behind-the-scenes prayer and sacrifice for them. "Love is patient," St. Paul says.[162]

---

[160] Elisabeth Leseur, *My Spirit Rejoices*.
[161] Acts 18:9-10.
[162] 1 Cor. 13:4.

Search and Rescue

Leave the rest in God's hands. Whether He sends a "Philip" into your sister-in-law's life to evangelize her, or whether she one day opens up and becomes willing to let you share the Faith with her, God will supply the necessary graces for her to come home to His Church. It may be that only in Heaven will your sister-in-law and your other non-Catholic family members realize that, all along and from afar, it was you who helped them get there.

Ask yourself now

• Am I patient with my family and courteous toward them?

• Have I tried to resolve and heal old wounds in my family, especially those wounds that I may have caused?

• Do I understand and accept with serenity the fact that in the wisdom of God's Providence I may not be the one He has chosen to reach my family members?

• Do I understand that, even if I'm not the one He uses for this task, I still have an obligation to share the Faith with my family and friends?

Search-and-rescue action agenda

• Pray for your family every day, just as St. Monica prayed for her wayward son, Augustine.

• Offer them encouragement and information, including good Catholic books, tapes, and pamphlets.

• Let your charitable patience, even in the face of their ridicule or rejection of the Faith, be a search-light to guide your non-Catholic family members home to the Church. This is how they'll know that you really do love Christ and that you're not merely out to win arguments.

• Be authentic and unpretentious in your Catholicism, and you'll stand a much better chance of winning your family over. Shun any temptation to be aggressive, pushy, or argumentative.

• Meditate on this exhortation of St. Paul: "Preach the word, be urgent in season and out of season, convince, rebuke, and exhort, be unfailing in patience and in teaching. . . . Always be steady, endure suffering, do the work of an evangelist, fulfill your ministry."[163]

[163] 2 Tim. 4:2, 5.

Search and Rescue

• End your meditations and resolutions with the following prayer:

O my God,
henceforth I resolve to strive
earnestly to be patient and gentle,
and not to allow the waters of contradiction
to extinguish the fire of that charity
that I owe to my neighbor.[164]

[164]*Manual of Prayers*, 64.

Chapter 9

Let God do the heavy lifting

"It is our part to seek,
His to grant what we ask;
ours to make a beginning,
His to bring it to completion;
ours to offer what we can,
His to finish what we cannot.

St. Jerome

There are many crucial elements to a successful search-and-rescue mission: preparation, prayer, listening, study, practice, patience, generosity, charity, humility, a spirit of boldness. These are all essential, but they aren't sufficient in themselves.

When you step forward in faith as an apostle and say, "Here I am, Lord. Send me," you must also be on guard against your own weaknesses and other hidden defects that can hinder your efforts to explain and share the Faith. Vainglory, resentment, jealousy, inordinate anger, fear, stubbornness: these and other spiritual "weeds" can spring up in your heart and choke off the vitality of your apostolic zeal for souls. You must uproot and eradicate these weeds by striving daily to cultivate the virtues of kindness, tact, gentleness, humility, and consideration for others.[165] Ask God to take

---

[165] *The Hidden Power of Kindness*, by Fr. Lawrence G. Lovaisk, will help you identify your weaknesses in these areas (and rid yourself of them, with God's help).

Search and Rescue

His heavenly "weed-whacker" of grace to these spiritual weeds in your soul. If you let Him, He'll help you eliminate or at least curb your defects and develop the virtues you need to carry out your mission as His apostle.[166]

But beyond all these necessities — things over which you and I can exert at least some control — there lies another, far more important factor: the will of God.

In ways you simply can't fathom, God's Providence and loving grace are at work in the lives of your family and friends (and in your own life). This is why you must always remember that, despite your best efforts to evangelize (as well as despite your worst failures), God's Providence is always active, directing on the path of grace the person you're trying to bring home.

Even in souls who seem bleak and lost, God is close at hand and His grace is active. Each time you encounter someone who needs to be drawn home to the Church, you stand face-to-face with a profound mystery: the hidden interplay

---

[166] As Christ said, "Why do you see the speck that is in your brother's eye, but do not notice the log that is in your own eye? Or how can you say to your brother, 'Let me take that speck out of your eye,' when there is a log in your eye? You hypocrite, first take the log out of your own eye, and then you will see clearly to take the speck out of your brother's eye" (Matt. 7:3-5).

between God's grace and that person's free will. Like Moses when God commanded him from the burning bush to remove his sandals because he was standing on holy ground,[167] in the presence of the mystery that is another human being — any other human being — you and I should experience a deep, joyful reverence.

~

God is calling you to sow the seed of truth

Why is it that some people hear the call of grace and convert to the Catholic Church while others don't? The answer is found in the Lord's parable of the sower. In it we see how truth takes root and grows in some souls and bears no fruit in others:

> A sower went out to sow. And as he sowed, some
> seeds fell along the path, and the birds came and
> devoured them. Other seeds fell on rocky ground,
> where they had not much soil, and immediately
> they sprang up, since they had no depth of soil,
> but when the sun rose they were scorched; and
> since they had no root they withered away. Other
> seeds fell upon thorns, and the thorns grew up and
> choked them. Other seeds fell on good soil and

[167] Cf. Exod. 3:5.

brought forth grain, some a hundredfold, some sixty, some thirty. He who has ears, let him hear. . . .

Hear, then, the parable of the sower. When anyone hears the word of the kingdom and does not understand it, the evil one comes and snatches away what is sown in his heart; this is what was sown along the path. As for what was sown on rocky ground, this is he who hears the word and immediately receives it with joy; yet he has no root in himself, but endures for a while, and when tribulation or persecution arises on account of the word, immediately he falls away. As for what was sown among thorns, this is he who hears the word, but the cares of the world and the delight in riches choke the word, and it proves unfruitful. As for what was sown on good soil, this is he who hears the word and understands it; he indeed bears fruit and yields, in one case a hundredfold, in another sixty, and in another thirty.[168]

Some people readily accept the truth; others reject it because the soil of their heart isn't ready for the seed you plant. Prejudices, ignorance, anger, and intellectual or moral laziness can all be factors that prevent the seed of

[168]Matt. 13: 3-9,18-23.

the Faith from taking root and bearing fruit in your friend's heart.

Perhaps you've done your best to share the Faith with her. Your best efforts seem to yield no results. She won't listen to you. She won't read the Catholic books you give her. She persists in her opposition to the Church.

What should you do now?

First, recall that you'll never be able to see and understand all the circumstances of your search-and-rescue mission; only God can see them. So commend your mission to God with faith and hope. Entrust your friend to Him, and do your best to share the Faith when she'll let you. Continue to be a beacon of goodness and charity to her.

Above all, don't become discouraged. Notice that, in Christ's parable, the job of the sower is to cast the seed and move on. His mission isn't to stand there, huddled over the grain of wheat, waiting anxiously to see whether it will take root and grow. That's God's task.

Because you have regular contact with her, you can't help but notice your friend's progress, or lack of it. But the key here is not to lose your peace over how things appear to be going. Whether you see results or not really isn't important. God sees what's happening in her soul. What He asks of you is to have faith in His grace and mercy and to be vigilant and generous in praying, doing your best to radiate the light of Christ in your actions and in your words.[169]

> I charge you in the presence of God and of Christ Jesus . . . preach the word, be urgent in season and out of season, convince, rebuke, and exhort, be unfailing in patience and in teaching.[170]

‍

God's ways are often beyond your understanding

You are the sower.

You sow the seed, and God follows behind with His grace to give the increase. He makes you His partner in the mystery of His Providence. But God is the one who converts hearts, not you or I. His grace can reach souls in ways we can't understand.

That's why ultimately, when it comes to explaining and sharing the Faith with others, you must not measure your success in terms of arguments won or converts made. This isn't a numbers game. Only God knows the hidden realities of the human heart. For that reason, situations that, to you, seem failures may in fact be, in God's eyes, victories of grace and truth.

[169]Cf. Matt. 5:14-16.
[170]2 Tim. 4:1-2.

Let God do the heavy lifting

I learned this lesson a few years ago, when I was in Chicago conducting apologetics seminars at several area parishes. On a free afternoon, I took the opportunity to visit my friend Bob, who's a Southern Baptist. We had spoken by phone and corresponded for over a year, and he had invited me over for a face-to-face discussion of the doctrinal issues that separate Catholics and Protestants. I saw this as a prime search-and-rescue opportunity. So I went, hoping that I'd be able to make some headway with him and bring him closer to the Catholic Church.

Now, if you're acquainted with Southern Baptists, you know that they're upright, devout Christians. They don't drink alcohol, they don't smoke, they don't dance, they don't gamble, and they don't play cards. In fact, many Southern Baptists I've met associate these activities with Catholics.

Bob was a likeable, friendly fellow who happened to be strongly opposed to Catholic teaching. He was a Bible-believing Christian who felt that the Catholic Church's teachings were wrong in many instances, and, whenever he had the opportunity, he used the Bible to point this out to any Catholic who'd listen. I was more than willing to listen to his case against the Catholic Church.

Over a pot of coffee, we sat in Bob's den with our Bibles open, engaged in a friendly but vigorous (at times heated) discussion about Catholic beliefs. Our exchange was typical of those between Evangelical Protestants and Catholics who are mutually interested in biblical truth. Over the course of the afternoon, we talked about several issues that Bob and other Protestants dispute with Catholics: Purgatory, the Real Presence of Christ in the Eucharist, and Mary. Eventually the discussion settled on the Communion of Saints.

Bob's arguments followed the standard Protestant objections to Catholic teaching on the role of Mary and the saints as intercessors for Christians on earth.[171] Over the course of an hour, we covered many biblical passages where I showed him that, far from being unbiblical, Catholic teaching on Mary and the saints is in fact the biblical position.

I grew bolder as I saw Bob backpedaling on this issue. As I pressed my arguments, I could see that he was gradually beginning to come around, agreeing that maybe the Catholic position had more merit than he had thought. I kept a calm exterior, but inside I was bursting with excitement. All of my clever biblical arguments were paying off!

Seeing an opportunity to press my advantage, I took a radical step. (What did I have to lose, after all? My arguments

[171] In my book *Any Friend of God's Is a Friend of Mine*, I provide a detailed biblical explanation of this issue and how you can discuss it with your Protestant friends.

were clearly overpowering Bob's flimsy Protestant arguments.) I invited him to go with me to an Eastern Catholic Church I knew of a few miles from his house. I had stopped there on my way to his place to make a visit to Christ in the Blessed Sacrament. I had seen some stupendously beautiful, floor-to-ceiling icons there, and one of them was a glorious image of the "cloud of witnesses," the saints in Heaven who watch us here on earth, spoken about in Hebrews 12:1.[172]

To my great and happy surprise, Bob said yes to my invitation to go to the Catholic church. "I've never been inside a Catholic church before," he admitted as we headed out in my rental car. I was elated! In addition to all my clever arguments and irrefutable logic I had pummeled him with that afternoon, I knew that my "double-whammy" secret weapon was waiting in the tabernacle of that church. Once I got Bob inside, not only would the beauty of the icons impress him, but the Blessed Sacrament, I knew, would bombard him with grace. I was sure God's grace would push him over the edge, completing all the careful work I had begun that afternoon.

When we arrived at the parish, we found the doors locked. We peered through the windows, but the dim interior of the

---

[172]Heb. 12:1 was one of the key biblical texts I used that afternoon to try to convince Bob of the Catholic teaching on the Communion of Saints.

church made it impossible for us to see, much less appreciate, the beautiful icons. Nonetheless I wasn't to be dissuaded from my search-and-rescue mission to save Bob from the clutches of his Southern Baptist objections to Catholicism.

I tugged on each door to no avail. The church was locked tight. As I rounded the corner in search of another door to try, I saw a man walk through a door into a building attached to the rear of the church. "Aha!" I thought to myself. "He's probably a janitor or maybe even one of the parish priests taking care of some odd job inside. He'll let us in, once I explain the reason for our visit."

My excitement grew.

The scene as we got to the door is etched in my mind. I turned to Bob with a smile, clapped him on the shoulder, and said, "This will be great, Bob. I really think you'll find these icons interesting and helpful in understanding the Catholic teaching on the Communion of Saints."

Bob smiled. "Yeah, I'm looking forward to this. As a Southern Baptist, I've never had any reason to go into a Catholic church before. This should be interesting."

I opened the door and came face-to-face with a large church hall full of several hundred Catholics . . . playing *bingo*.

I groaned inwardly. "No, Lord, not now!"

Let God do the heavy lifting

The first thing that struck us was the raucous noise of the gambling. Shouts, hoots, guffaws, and cackles rippled through the room. These Catholic gamblers were into the game, oblivious to anything except their chance of winning that pot of money. The next thing that hit us was the wave of cigarette smoke billowing out. Nearly everyone, it seemed, had a cigarette dangling from his lips.

Bob and I stood in the doorway, frozen.

A portly man waddled by with four large plastic cups of beer in each hand, gripped by his fingertips. There was no way to know whether all eight beers were for him or whether he was bringing some to share with his tablemates.

The smoking, the gambling, the drinking, the whooping and hollering, the carousing! I was mortified. Bob was overwhelmed by this kaleidoscope of Catholic scandal. All his prejudices against Catholics were inflamed and confirmed in that instant. It was as if I had opened the gates of Hell in front of my Southern Baptist pal and said, "Welcome to the Catholic Church, Bob!"

Have you ever seen a large building being demolished by dynamite?

In just a few seconds, the whole marvelous edifice collapses in a heap of rubble. Well, that's what happened with Bob in that moment. In spite of all my biblical progress earlier that day, Bob had just come face-to-face with what he saw to be Catholic Bingo Hell, and it destroyed any Catholic biblical edifice I may have built earlier.

We managed finally to find a way into the church itself, looked at the icons for a few minutes, then got back in the car for an awkward drive back to his house. I didn't know what to say, and he was embarrassed for me.

⌒

Learn to rely on God

This episode taught me a huge lesson, one that I want to share with you so you can avoid the mistake I made that day. That afternoon I had been so sure, so confident (and so wrong) about my own ability to persuade Bob with my intellectual and biblical arguments. But God used that opportunity to show me how wrong I was. Don't make the same mistake I made with Bob. Don't think you can change a person's heart through your efforts alone. Without God's will and help, even your best efforts are bound to fail. You must learn to rely on God.

Remember that it's God who has to do the heavy lifting when it comes to changing a person's heart. Only He is able to illuminate hearts and minds with the light of His grace. In my experience with Bob, I realized with chagrin that I had been relying on my own powers of persuasion. It wasn't the

Holy Spirit's timing for Bob to come into the Church. If anything, the whole episode was most likely the Lord's way of knocking me down a few pegs, showing me that I'm called to be a sower of his seed, but He's the master of the harvest.

And we can thank Him for that! If the conversion of souls were our job, and not His, few people would ever come to Christ and into His Church. The Bible tells us to say, "Speak, Lord, Your servant is listening."[173] But it's not hard to become blinded by our own ego and vainglory to the point at which we're really saying, "Listen, Lord. Your servant is speaking." That's exactly the wrong-headed attitude I had adopted with Bob that day. And I'm grateful that Christ showed it to me.

So I'll say it again: Let God do the heavy lifting.

As you embark on your search-and-rescue missions, remember this important teaching of Christ: "I am the vine, you are the branches. He who abides in me, and I in him, he it is that bears much fruit, for apart from me you can do nothing. If a man does not abide in me, he is cast forth as a branch and withers; and the branches are gathered, thrown into the fire, and burned. If you abide in me, and my words abide in you, ask whatever you will, and it shall be done for you."[174]

---

[173]Cf. 1 Sam. 3:9.
[174]John 15:5-7.

Search and Rescue

Let the truth of Christ's words sink deep into your heart so they can animate your efforts to be a search-and-rescue apostle. Apart from Him, you can do nothing. The corollary is also true: "What is impossible with men is possible with God."[175]

Ask yourself now

• Do I pray for guidance in my search-and-rescue missions, or do I act impulsively?

• In my search-and-rescue efforts, do I understand that I'm only God's messenger? Do I do all I can and leave the results to God?

• Do I trust that God can achieve results through me even though my efforts are modest and simple?

Search-and-rescue agenda

• Pray for the virtue of humility.

• Ask God to help you overcome your spiritual defects and to show you what He wants you to do in your search-and-rescue mission.

[175]Luke 18:27.

Let God do the heavy lifting

• Resolve not to look for results. Only God knows the hidden workings of souls. What look like failures to you may in fact be victories for grace and truth in God's eyes.

• Meditate on this passage from Proverbs: "Trust in the Lord with all your heart, and do not rely on your own insight. In all your ways acknowledge Him, and He will make straight your paths."[176]

• End your meditations and resolutions with the following prayer:

Lord Jesus,
I give You my hands to do Your work.
I give You my feet to go Your way.
I give You my eyes to see as You see.
I give You my tongue to speak Your words.
I give You my mind to think as You think.
I give You my spirit so that You may pray in me.
I give You myself so that You may grow in me.
So that it is You, Lord Jesus, who lives
and works and prays in me. Amen.[177]

[176]Prov. 3:5-6.
[177]*Manual of Prayers*, 81.

Epilogue

"You are standing in front of God
and in the presence of the holy angels.
The Holy Spirit is about to impress His seal
on your soul. You are about to be pressed
into the service of the great King."

St. Cyril of Jerusalem

A man was walking along the shore one morning. A storm had battered the coast the day before, and now the beach was littered with driftwood, fish, shells, and other debris churned up by the waves. As the man walked, he caught sight of a little girl in the distance; she was stooping to collect things and then throwing them into the waves. "She's probably skipping rocks or shells in the waves," the man thought. But he was wrong. When he drew closer, he could see that the girl was picking up starfish, one at a time, and throwing them back into the water. There were thousands of starfish washed up on the sand.

"Little girl," the man called to her with a chuckle, "why are you throwing those starfish back?"

"I'm saving their lives." She said. "If I leave them here on the sand, they'll die. But if I throw them back into the water, they'll live."

"But there are thousands of these dying starfish! You'll never save them all. Why bother? What does it matter?"

Search and Rescue

She smiled and held up one starfish, admiring its colors in the light of the sun. "Well, it sure matters to *this* one."

Then she tossed it into the waves and went on with her work.

⁀

Search-and-rescue missions to your family, friends, coworkers, and even strangers are a lot like the girl and the starfish. Some may scoff at you, wondering why you bother to try to draw souls into — or back into — the Church. After all there are so many "unsaved" people out there, billions of them. So why bother? What can you do to make a difference in this world? No matter how hard you try, no matter how many people you might reach, it's still just an infinitesimally small drop in the bucket. Right?

Wrong.

God doesn't see things that way; nor should you. Christ didn't come to save us as a herd. He came to save each of us individually. Christ is person-specific in His search-and-rescue mission to you and to me.

It's true, given the enormous quantity of people who need to be rescued with His message of truth and love and life, that you'll likely be able to reach out to only a very few of them.

So what?

Like the girl who was rescuing the starfish, you must look at each of your family members and friends with the same sort of person-specific love and concern. When you feel discouraged or ineffective, remember what the little girl said: "It matters to *this* one."

Christ told us how He views our efforts to help those around us, even if our efforts are modest and simple. In His eyes, your loving concern for the spiritual welfare of your family and friends, for their salvation, has immense value. If caring for their physical needs is important to the Lord, how much more important to Him will be your spiritual efforts on their behalf.

You minister to Christ Himself
when you reach out to others

Spend a few moments meditating prayerfully on Christ's words in the following passage and recognize that here Christ explains the search-and-rescue mission He has given you.

When the Son of Man comes in His glory, and all the angels with Him, then He will sit on His glorious throne. Before Him will be gathered all the nations, and He will separate them one from another as a shepherd separates the sheep from the goats, and He

will place the sheep at His right hand, but the goats
at the left. Then the King will say to those at His
right hand, "Come, O blessed of my Father, inherit
the kingdom prepared for you from the foundation of
the world; for I was hungry and you gave me food, I
was thirsty and you gave me drink, I was a stranger
and you welcomed me, I was naked and you clothed
me, I was sick and you visited me, I was in prison and
you came to me."

Then the righteous will answer Him, "Lord, when
did we see Thee hungry and feed Thee, or thirsty and
give Thee drink? And when did we see Thee a stranger
and welcome Thee, or naked and clothe Thee? And
when did we see Thee sick or in prison and visit Thee?"
And the King will answer them, "Truly, I say to you,
as you did it to one of the least of these my brethren,
you did it to me."

Then He will say to those at His left hand, "Depart
from me, you cursed, into the eternal fire prepared for
the Devil and his angels; for I was hungry and you gave
me no food, I was thirsty and you gave me no drink,
I was a stranger and you did not welcome me, naked
and you did not clothe me, sick and in prison and you
did not visit me."

Then they also will answer, "Lord, when did we see
Thee hungry or thirsty or a stranger or naked or sick
or in prison, and did not minister to Thee?" Then He
will answer them, "Truly, I say to you, as you did it not
to one of the least of these, you did it not to me."

And they will go away into eternal punishment,
but the righteous into eternal life.[178]

Do you see from this passage how important each soul is
to Christ? No matter who the person is, no matter how far
from the Church he may be, no matter how steeped in sin
or animosity toward the Church he may be, Christ is asking
you to help Him. Will you?

He wants to give you all the graces you need to cover
the nakedness of ignorance with the garment of truth, to
give spiritual nourishment to those who hunger and thirst
for forgiveness of their sins and to be reconciled with Christ
and His Church, and to visit the imprisoned — those who
live in spiritual exile from their true home, the Church.
Whether through circumstances of birth and upbringing or
because of a willful refusal to enter the Church Christ established, there are many people — many people you know personally — who live in a prison of separation from Christ and

[178]Matt. 25:31-46.

His Church. Christ is calling you by name to visit these people, to seek them out, and to liberate them.

⌒

Christ will give you all you need

Now that you've completed this book, you may feel strengthened to go out and begin your own search-and-rescue missions to your family and friends. (I hope you do!) You may have gained confidence because you now know some techniques and tools that will help you be more effective as an apostle for Christ.

But you also may still feel daunted by the task ahead.

So many people, so many arguments against the Church! All the emotions involved in your family relationships that complicate your efforts to reach out to your relatives: these and other obstacles loom. I don't want to suggest that they're not real obstacles. Knowing the basic search-and-rescue techniques makes your work much easier, but it won't ever be easy.

Take a moment. Lift your gaze. Don't you see that above all these human difficulties and obstacles hovers the Cross of Christ? Exclaim with St. Paul, "I can do all things in Him who strengthens me!"[179] Christ has promised His grace and strength to you; you need only ask Him for it.

[179]Phil. 4:13.

In spite of the boost I hope this book has given you, you may still wonder how you can personally make a difference. You may, even now, find those old excuses welling up inside you: "I'm not trained in theology or public speaking." "I have no background in explaining and defending the Faith." "I'm too old, too young, too shy." "I'll do it some other time." "I'm not prepared." "Who am I that I should be the one to talk about the Faith with my family and friends?"

Resist those temptations. Christ needs you, and He needs you now! He says to you what He said to Moses long ago, "I will be with you."

Recall the episode in the Gospels where Christ wants to feed thousands of people. You'll see yourself reflected there in the words and actions of the Apostles.

In those days, when again a great crowd had gathered, and they had nothing to eat, He called His disciples to Him and said to them, "I have compassion on the crowd, because they have been with me now three days, and have nothing to eat; and if I send them away hungry to their homes, they will faint on the way; and some of them have come a long way."

And His disciples answered Him, "How can one feed these men with bread here in the desert?"

Search and Rescue

And He asked them, "How many loaves have you?"
They said, "Seven." And He commanded the crowd
to sit down on the ground; and He took the seven
loaves, and having given thanks, He broke them and
gave them to His disciples to set before the people; and
they set them before the crowd. And they had a few
small fish; and having blessed them, He commanded
that these also should be set before them. [All the peo-
ple] ate and were satisfied; and they took up the broken pieces left over, seven baskets full. And there
were about four thousand people.[180]

Today our own situation is like that of the disciples.
People everywhere — people you and I meet in our daily
lives — are starving for the truth. They're spiritually fam-
ished because they don't know Jesus Christ and His Church.
You can feed them.

"But how can I feed them?" you ask, as did Christ's disciples. "I have no training. And besides, this culture we live in
is a spiritual wasteland. There's so much corruption and evil;
so many Catholics giving bad example."

Imagine the Apostles looking around in bewilderment at
the arid, empty landscape, rolling their eyes and wondering

[180]Mark 8:1-9; cf. Luke 9:12-17; John 6:1-14.

how in the world Christ could expect them to feed those thousands of people. Perhaps you feel that way right now.

In that moment, Christ required very little from His disciples. They managed to scrounge up a few loaves of bread and some dried fish, but that was enough for Christ to feed thousands of hungry people.

Likewise, when He asks you to help Him feed the spiritually hungry, He doesn't require much from you. All He asks for are the "loaves and fishes" in your life: your willingness to be a search-and-rescue apostle and your talents and abilities, however meager they may be.

If you offer Him your humble loaves and fishes, Christ will work miracles of grace and conversion through you. Don't be afraid or discouraged by the challenges you'll face. Christ has already assured you His loving grace can conquer even the hardest of hearts. So even if your loved ones are so entrenched in their opposition to the Catholic Church that winning them over seems impossible, remember that "with men it is impossible, but not with God; for all things are possible with God."[181]

Now go forth joyfully as a search-and-rescue apostle for Christ. Your family and friends are waiting for you.

[181] Mark 10:27.

Search-and-rescue
reading plan

Following is a selection of books you should read, depending on your level of proficiency in apologetics, doctrine, and Scripture. If you read one book a week, or every two weeks, you can move to deeper levels rather quickly. As you follow this reading plan, your knowledge and confidence will dramatically increase.

Keep in mind two things: First, these recommended resources should be added to your regular reading of Scripture and the *Catechism*; second, there are many other excellent books and tapes available to you. These are simply some of the many I recommend. Start with these, but be sure to read widely among different authors. I particularly recommend these publishers: Sophia Institute Press, Ignatius Press, and Our Sunday Visitor.

Phase 1 (Preliminary)

An Introduction to the Devout Life, by St. Francis de Sales.

This master of the spiritual life shows you in this book

the steps to achieving holiness and peace of mind. Before you can share Christ with others, you need to know, love, and serve Him yourself. This book shows you exactly how to do it and do it well.

Theology for Beginners, by Frank Sheed. This volume gives you a crash course in the basics of the Catholic Faith. It's very accessible, written for a popular audience, and one of the most helpful introductory books I know of. (Servant Books)

The Belief of Catholics, by Ronald Knox. This book shows clearly the contrasts between Catholicism and Protestantism. You'll find lots of easy-to-understand information here that will help you help others come home. (Ignatius Press)

The Hidden Power of Kindness, by Lawrence G. Lovasik. This indispensable book will guide you along the path of charity. It's a masterpiece of practical wisdom on everyday acts of virtue such as holding your temper, being kind, and putting up with others' defects. (Sophia Institute Press)

The Aquinas Catechism, by St. Thomas Aquinas. Learn the basics of the Catholic Faith from a master theologian — simple but profound catechetics. (Sophia Institute Press)

Where Is That in the Bible? by Patrick Madrid. This handbook of apologetics covers more than fifty aspects of the

Faith, including the Eucharist, Mary, the Pope, Purgatory, and the divinity of Christ, and gives you all the relevant Bible verses to assist you in your own study of the Bible and in your conversations with others. (Our Sunday Visitor Press)

Preparing Yourself for Mass, by Romano Guardini. The Mass is the centerpiece of your prayer life, and in this book you'll learn how to get the most out of it; it teaches you how to concentrate, how to pray well, and how to worship God with your whole heart, mind, and soul. (Sophia Institute Press)

Hind's Feet on High Places, by Hannah Hurnard. This delightful, deeply insightful, and inspiring allegory shows how a hesitant, complacent, bashful person can find the courage and determination to follow Christ's call, even if it means traveling difficult paths to reach Him. (Blacksmith Publishing)

Surprised by Truth 2, edited by Patrick Madrid. This collection of fifteen personal accounts of conversion and reconversion is packed with apologetics and has been responsible for many conversions to the Catholic Faith. (Sophia Institute Press)

Catholicism and Fundamentalism, by Karl Keating. This indispensable guide to dealing with aggressive Fundamentalist

Protestants who seek to convert Catholics covers a wide
variety of biblical and historical issues that are likely to
come up in such circumstances. (Ignatius Press)

A Guide to the Bible, by Antonio Fuentes. This succinct overview explains the background, structure, and purpose of
each book of the Bible. (Scepter Press)

The Fathers of the Church, by Mike Aquilina. Learn what the
early Christians believed and taught. This handy little
volume will round out your understanding of the Church
Fathers. (Our Sunday Visitor Press)

A Father Who Keeps His Promises, by Scott Hahn. This is a
good biblical explanation of the covenant God has with
His people and how that covenant has been perfected in
Christ and the Catholic Church. (Servant Publications)

How to Win an Argument, by Michael A. Gilbert. This book
will show you how to spot common fallacies in argumentation and how to refute them. This is a purely secular
book, but it will help you in your religious discussions.
(John Wiley and Sons)

Catholic Answers Complete Apologetics Tract Set (150
tracts on dozens of subjects). These brief tracts cover
virtually every conceivable issue that can come up in
discussions with non-Catholics. (www.catholic.com;
619-387-7200)

Envoy magazine. This award-winning Catholic magazine of apologetics is regarded by many as the leading magazine of its kind. *Envoy's* rich graphics, humor, and articles from today's top Catholic writers will supply you with a wealth of practical information on the Catholic Faith and will make your study enjoyable as well as profitable. (www.envoymagazine.com; 1-800-55-ENVOY)

Speak the Truth in Love, by Patrick Madrid (six audiotapes). These tapes offer a variety of helpful tips and techniques on sharing the Faith. (www.envoymagazine.com; 1-800-553-6869)

Handling Difficult Questions (four audiotapes). This set covers standard objections to the papacy, Mary, salvation, and more. (www.envoymagazine.com; 1-800-553-6869)

Defending the Faith, by Patrick Madrid (two audiotapes). With warm, humorous, practical examples, these tapes teach you the *dos* and *don'ts* of sharing the Faith. (www.envoymagazine.com; 1-800-553-6869)

New Advent supersite. This is an excellent Catholic portal that gives you direct, online access to a treasure-trove of information about the Catholic Faith, including the classic 1915 *Catholic Encyclopedia*, the Bible, Church documents, the writings of the Church Fathers, and other

Search and Rescue

tools to help you in your search-and-rescue missions. (www.newadvent.org)

☞

Phase 2 (Intermediate)

One, Holy, Catholic, and Apostolic, by Kenneth Whitehead. Here's an excellent introduction to the early Church, showing that in her beliefs, Liturgy, and practices, the early Church was the Catholic Church. (Ignatius Press)

Saint Edmund Campion, by Evelyn Waugh. This is the exciting story of an apologist and priest who converted from Protestantism and then conducted his own search-and-rescue missions in Elizabethan England, even in the face of death. It's a rousing story by a master novelist, and an example for us all. (Sophia Institute Press)

My Spirit Rejoices, by Elisabeth Leseur. Here's the inspiring diary of a Catholic woman whose atheistic husband tried every trick he could think of to pry her loose from her faith in Christ. He failed. After her death, he read this diary, converted to the Catholic Faith, and became a priest. (Sophia Institute Press)

Theology and Sanity, by Frank Sheed. This classic brings clarity and light to every discussion as it explains at a deeper level the reasons behind Catholic teachings, making sense of doctrines that can puzzle even committed, well-catechized Catholics. (Ignatius Press)

Fundamentals of the Faith, by Peter Kreeft. A lucid explanation of Catholic teaching compared with Islam, Hinduism, and Buddhism, this book will expand your understanding of how Christianity fares when its claims are measured against those of other religions. (Ignatius Press)

Pope Fiction, by Patrick Madrid. Here are penetrating answers to thirty myths and misconceptions about the papacy, including biblical and historical arguments. (Basilica Press)

The Shepherd and the Rock, by J. Michael Miller, C.S.B. Using a popular yet somewhat academic approach, the author supplies you with a wealth of information about the theological and biblical foundations of the papacy and how it has developed and been perpetuated in the life of the Catholic Church. (Our Sunday Visitor Press)

The Lamb's Supper, by Scott Hahn. This book will deepen your understanding of and love for the Holy Sacrifice of the Mass. It explores the riches of the Sacred Liturgy as it's mysteriously revealed in the Letter to the Hebrews and the Book of Revelation. Read it not only for your own benefit and sanctification, but also so you'll be able to explain the Mass better to your non-Catholic friends. (Doubleday)

Search and Rescue

A Handbook of Christian Apologetics, by Ronald Tacelli,
S.J., and Peter Kreeft. This is the most comprehensive,
most useful, and most irrefutable collection of Catholic
apologetics arguments in a single volume in the area of
atheism, the "problem of evil," the divinity of Christ, and
related issues. Your efforts to reach atheists and agnostics
will be greatly enhanced if you study this wonderful book.
(InterVarsity Press)

Catholic for a Reason, by Scott Hahn, Leon J. Suprenant, Jr.,
et al. These two volumes cover the biblical evidence for
Catholic teachings on the Church, Mary, the Mass, Purgatory, and salvation. Each gives you many solid biblical
references that will help you help others see that the
Catholic Church is the church that Christ established.
(Emmaus Road Publishing)

The Gentle Art of Verbal Self-Defense, by Suzette Haden
Elgin. This book will school you in the "gentle" art of
dealing well with tense situations and give you proven
techniques to keep you from getting trapped or stymied
by the arguments and "attack speech" used by belligerent
or domineering people. Before you try to defend the
Faith in the face of your obstinate or aggressive non-
Catholic friends and relatives, read this book! (Prentice-
Hall Press)

Search-and-rescue reading plan

The Hidden Manna, by Fr. James T. O'Connor. This biblical
and historical explanation of the Catholic doctrine of the
Holy Eucharist covers its New Testament origin, its development in the early Church, and the various heresies
raised against it over the centuries, including those that
emerged during the Protestant rebellion. (Ignatius Press)

Any Friend of God's Is a Friend of Mine, by Patrick Madrid.
This book will supply you with all the biblical information you need to explain to Protestants the Catholic doctrine of the Communion of Saints, including honoring
and praying to Mary and the saints, praying for the souls
in Purgatory, and the Catholic use of statues and icons.
(Basilica Press)

Hail, Holy Queen, by Scott Hahn. This book covers the
basics of Marian theology using Scripture as a guide and
shows you how to explain Catholic teachings about Mary
to your Protestant friends. (Doubleday)

St. Cyril of Jerusalem on the Sacraments. Here's the teaching
of the Catholic Church on the sacraments as it was delivered to Christians in the third and fourth centuries! This
is a powerful tool for proving to Protestants that the early
Christians were Catholic. (St. Vladimir's Seminary Press)

The Faith of the Early Fathers, edited by William Jurgens.
This three-volume set is indispensable: it gives you the

complete array of Church teaching, broken down by
topic, as it appears in the writings of the Church Fathers.
With this set, you'll be able to prove that Catholic doctrines were present in the early Church. (The Liturgical
Press)

The Splendor of the Church, by Henri de Lubac. In these
pages, de Lubac will help you see that the Church, in
spite of defects in her members and difficult problems she
faces, is the Church that Christ established and contin-
ues to guard. (Ignatius Press)

Not by Scripture Alone, by Robert Sungenis, Patrick Madrid,
et al. This book will help you in your discussions with
Protestants on the subject of *sola scriptura*. Covering an
exhaustive array of biblical and historical data, this powerful book leaves no Protestant argument on this subject
unanswered. (Queenship)

An Introduction to Catholic Social Teaching, Fr. Rodger
Charles, S.J. This book will get you up to speed on what
the Catholic Church teaches on social issues. Some non-
Catholics are drawn to the Church when they discover
her teachings as they affect the poor and the working-
man. (Ignatius Press)

Salvation Outside the Church? by Francis Sullivan, S.J. This
useful presentation of the Catholic teaching on salvation

outside the Church gives you the historical background
of this sometimes controversial subject and shows how
the Church's past statements can be harmonized with
more recent statements by Pope Pius XII and Vatican II.
(Paulist Press)

Charles de Foucauld, by Jean-Jacques Antier. This inspiring
account of a Frenchman who became a search-and-rescue
apostle (and martyr) to Muslims in Northern Africa will
teach you how to build bridges to people who strongly
resist your message. (Ignatius Press)

Liturgical Question Box, by Msgr. Peter Elliott. Here's an
excellent book that will answer all your questions about
how Mass should be celebrated — what's allowed and
what isn't. (Ignatius Press)

Handbook of Denominations in the United States, by Frank
Spencer Mead. This book, compiled by a Protestant, is a
handy guide for Catholics who want to understand the
basics of Protestant denominations and how doctrinally
fragmented they are. (Abingdon Press)

☞

Phase 3 (Advanced)

Fundamentals of Catholic Dogma, by Ludwig Ott. This indispensable book gives you a comprehensive, systematic presentation of virtually all aspects of the Catholic Faith,

including biblical and historical references that support
Catholic teaching. (TAN Books)

All Generations Shall Call Me Blessed, by Stefano Manelli.
This book provides a good overview of the historical
and biblical evidence supporting Catholic Marian doctrines. (Academy of the Immaculate)

An Essay on the Development of Christian Doctrine, by the
Venerable John Henry Newman. This classic shows
how Catholic teaching develops over the course of
history. (University of Notre Dame Press)

A History of the Church, by Philip Hughes. One of the
best compact histories of the Catholic Church I know
of, this volume is detailed but readable and very helpful for getting the "big picture." (Sheed and Ward,
London)

Patrology, by Johannes Quasten. This four-volume collection of writings from the Church Fathers (including
background information on them and the particulars of
their individual milieus) will take you to the next level,
after you've gone through Jurgens's set (see Phase 2).
(Thomas More Press)

Basics of Biblical Greek, by William D. Mounce. For the
advanced search-and-rescue apostle, learning the basics
of biblical Greek will be a strong asset. This book is a

standard college-level introduction to New Testament Greek. It's easy to follow, and you can learn to read biblical Greek at your own pace. (Zondervan)

Mary, a History of Doctrine and Devotion, by Hilda Graef. This large, detailed book on the two-thousand-year development of Marian teaching and devotion is deep but not at all dry or difficult. (Sheed and Ward, London)

The Spirit of Catholicism, by Karl Adam. Here's a superb book for explaining the mystique of Catholicism to non-Catholics, especially Protestants. It covers doctrine, authority, and spirituality in a clear, convincing, charitable style. (Franciscan University Press)

The Christian Faith in the Doctrinal Documents of the Catholic Church, edited by J. Neuner, S.J., and J. Dupuis, S.J. This reference book shows you when and where Catholic doctrines were first formally taught by the Catholic Church. It's a great companion to *Where Is That in the Bible?* (Phase 1) and *Fundamentals of Catholic Dogma* (Phase 2). (Alba House)

A History of Christendom, by Warren Carroll. This four-volume Church history is perhaps the best available today in English. (Three more volumes are planned.) Extremely well-written, well-organized, and well-documented, this vibrant history gives you a magnificent view of the Church. (Christendom College Press)

The Spirit and Forms of Protestantism, by Fr. Louis Bouyer. If you really want to understand what makes Protestants "tick," read this book. In it, Fr. Bouyer, a convert to the Catholic Church, takes you on a guided tour inside Protestantism. He helps you see how and why Protestants approach Scripture the way they do and what you as a Catholic should know to draw them home to the Church. (Scepter Press)

Biographical note

Patrick Madrid

Patrick Madrid is the founder and publisher of the award-winning *Envoy* magazine, a leading Catholic journal of apologetics and evangelization. A best-selling author, he has written several books, including *Surprised by Truth, Surprised by Truth 2, Any Friend of God's Is a Friend of Mine, Pope Fiction, Where Is That in the Bible?, Not by Scripture Alone* (which he co-authored with Robert Sungenis et al.) and *Surprised by Life*, forthcoming from Sophia Institute Press®. He's also a contributor to the *Ignatius Encyclopedia of Apologetics*.

In addition to writing books and articles on apologetics, Madrid has conducted hundreds of apologetics conferences in English and Spanish across the United States, as well as in Europe, Asia, Latin America, and the Middle East. He's a veteran of numerous public debates on religious issues with Protestant ministers, Mormon leaders, and other non-Catholic spokesmen.

He also hosts two popular EWTN television series: "Pope Fiction" and "The Truth About Scripture and Tradition."

Search and Rescue

Patrick, his wife, Nancy, and their eleven children live in the countryside of central Ohio.

Patrick Madrid is available for speaking engagements at your parish. Information on his apologetics and evangelization parish seminars is available on the Internet at www.envoymagazine.com/seminar.htm. Contact him by e-mail at patrickmadrid@hotmail.com or at P.O. Box 640, Granville, OH 43023; fax: 740-928-5975.

Sophia Institute Press®

Sophia Institute™ is a nonprofit institution that seeks to restore man's knowledge of eternal truth, including man's knowledge of his own nature, his relation to other persons, and his relation to God.

Sophia Institute Press® serves this end in numerous ways: it publishes translations of foreign works to make them accessible for the first time to English-speaking readers; it brings out-of-print books back into print; and it publishes important new books that fulfill the ideals of Sophia Institute™. These books afford readers a rich source of the enduring wisdom of mankind.

Sophia Institute Press® makes these high-quality books available to the general public by using advanced technology and by soliciting donations to subsidize its general publishing costs.

Your generosity can help Sophia Institute Press® to provide the public with editions of works containing the enduring wisdom of the ages. Please send your tax-deductible contribution to the address below. We also welcome your questions, comments, and suggestions.

For your free catalog, call:
Toll-free: 1-800-888-9344

or write:
Sophia Institute Press®
Box 5284, Manchester, NH 03108

or visit our website:
www.sophiainstitute.com

Sophia Institute™ is a tax-exempt institution
as defined by the Internal Revenue Code,
Section 501(c)(3). Tax I.D. 22-2548708.